THIR[

DAYS

OF HEALING

Living in the Fullness of God's Purposes.

SCOTT REECE

kindle
direct
publishing

Published by Kindle Direct a division of Amazon Publishing

Seattle, Washington, www.kdp.amazon.com

ISBN: 9781518649486

Library of Congress Cataloging-in-Publication Data is on file at the Library of Congress, Washington, DC.

Table of Contents

DEDICATION

No man can truly claim credit for who he is. Many people have invested into my life and I am the sum total of those investments.

This book is dedicated to the many mentors who have faithfully and patiently shaped my life. Gratefully, my life is the result of theirs.

This book was lovingly written for my children: Jessica, Jordan, Lauren, Joseph, Kate, and Isabella. May the Word of Life, guard you and guide you each, all the days of your lives.

Finally, I dedicate this to the love of my life: Michelle. You have saved me.

One Hundred Scriptures on Faith

What does the Word say about Health, Healing and Wholeness? Sickness is never the will of God and the Word reveals that the Father longs for you to *always* be healthy. As you read this book, rise up, embrace the Word, let it become truth and life in your spirit, in your mind and in your reality. Let the Word flow into your spirit and healing will flow out of your spirit and into your body. When His Word becomes alive on the inside of you, it will transform every part of which you are, spirit, soul and body. Let the seed of the Word take root, stand in faith without wavering and as the seed begins to grow, you will partake of the fruit and many others will "taste and see that the Lord is good."

Old Testament

1. I am the Lord that heals you (Exodus 15:26).

2. You shall be buried in a good old age (Genesis 15:15).

3. You shall come to your grave in a full age like as a shock of corn comes in its season (Job 5:26).

4. When I see the blood, I will pass over you and the plague shall not be upon you to destroy you (Exodus 12:13).

5. I will take sickness away from the midst of you and the number

of your days I will fulfill (Exodus 23:25-26).

6. I will not put any of the diseases you are afraid of on you, but I will take all sickness away from you (Deuteronomy 7:15).

7. It will be well with you and your days shall be multiplied and prolonged as the days of heaven upon the earth (Deuteronomy 11:9, 21).

8. I turned the curse into a blessing unto you, because I loved you (Deuteronomy 23:5 and Nehemiah 13:2).

9) I have redeemed you from every sickness and every plague (Deuteronomy 28:61 and Galatians 3:13).

10. As your days, so shall your strength be (Deuteronomy 33:25).

11. I have found a ransom for you; your flesh shall be fresher than a child's and you shall return to the days of your youth (Job 33:24-25).

12. I have healed you and brought up your soul from the grave; I have kept you alive from going down into the pit (Psalm 30:1-2).

13. I will give you strength and bless you with peace (Psalm 29:11).

14. I will preserve you and keep you alive (Psalm 41:2).

15. I will strengthen you upon the bed of languishing; I will turn all your bed in your sickness (Psalm 41:3).

16. I am the health of your countenance and your God (Psalm 43:5).

17. No plague shall come near your dwelling (Psalm 91:10).

18. I will satisfy you with long life (Psalm 91:16).

19. I heal all your diseases (Psalm 103:3).

20. I sent My word and healed you and delivered you from your destructions (Psalm 107:20).

21. You shall not die, but live, and declare My works (Psalm 118:17).

22. I heal your broken heart and bind up your wounds (Psalm 147:3).

23. The years of your life shall be many (Proverbs 4:10).

24. Trusting Me brings health to your navel and marrow to your bones (Proverbs 3:8).

25. My words are life to you, and health/medicine to all your flesh (Proverbs 4:22).

26. (My) good report makes your bones fat (Proverbs 15:30).

27. (My) pleasant words are sweet to your soul and health to your bones (Proverbs 16:24).

28. My joy is your strength. A merry heart does good like a medicine (Nehemiah 8:10; Proverbs 17:22).

29. The eyes of the blind shall be opened. The eyes of them that see shall not be dim (Isaiah 32:3; 35:5).

30. The ears of the deaf shall be unstopped. The ears of them that hear shall hearken (Isaiah 32:3; 35:5).

31. The tongue of the dumb shall sing. The tongue of those that stammer shall be ready to speak plainly (Isaiah 35:6; 32:4).

32. The lame man shall leap as a hart (Isaiah 35:6).

33. I will recover you and make you to live. I am ready to save you (Isaiah 38:16, 20).

34. I give power to the faint. I increase strength to them that have no might (Isaiah 40:29).

35. I will renew your strength. I will strengthen and help you (Isaiah 40:31; 41:10).

36. To your old age and gray hairs I will carry you and I will deliver you (Isaiah 46:4).

37. I bore your sickness (Isaiah 53:4).

38. I carried your pains (Isaiah 53:4).

39. I was put to sickness for you (Isaiah 53:10).

40. With My stripes you are healed (Isaiah 53:5).

41. I will heal you (Isaiah 57:19).

42. Your light shall break forth as the morning and your health shall spring forth speedily (Isaiah 58:8).

43. I will restore health unto you, and I will heal you of your wounds says the Lord (Jeremiah 30:17).

44. Behold I will bring it health and cure, and I will cure you, and will reveal unto you the abundance of peace and truth (Jeremiah 33:6).

45. I will bind up that which was broken and will strengthen that which was sick (Ezekiel 34:16).

46. Behold, I will cause breath to enter into you and you shall live. And I shall put My Spirit in you and you shall live (Ezekiel 37:5, 14).

47. Whithersoever the rivers shall come shall live. They shall be

healed, and everything shall live where the river comes (Ezekiel 47:9).

48. Seek Me and you shall live (Amos 5:4, 6).

49. I have arisen with healing in My wings (Malachi 4:2).

New Testament

50. I will, be thou clean (Matthew 8:3).

51. I took your infirmities (Matthew 8:17).

52. I bore your sicknesses (Matthew 8:17).

53. If you're sick you need a physician. (I am the Lord your physician) (Matthew 9:12 & Exodus 15:26).

54. I am moved with compassion toward the sick and I heal them (Matthew 14:14).

55. I heal all manner of sickness and all manner of disease (Matthew 4:23).

56. According to your faith, be it unto you (Matthew 9:29).

57. I give you power and authority over all unclean spirits to cast them out, and to heal all manner of sickness and all manner of disease (Matthew 10:1 & Luke 9:1).

58. I heal them all (Matthew 12:15 & Hebrews 13:8).

59. As many as touch Me are made perfectly whole (Matthew 14:36).

60. Healing is the children's bread (Matthew 15:26).

61. I do all things well. I make the deaf to hear and the dumb to speak (Mark 7:37).

62. If you can believe, all things are possible to him that believeth (Mark 9:23; 11:23-24).

63. When hands are laid on you, you shall recover (Mark 16:18).

64. My anointing heals the brokenhearted, and delivers the captives, recovers sight to the blind, and sets at liberty those that are bruised (Luke 4:18; Isaiah 10:27; 61:1).

65. I heal all those who have need of healing (Luke 9:11).

66. I am not come to destroy men's lives but to save them (Luke 9:56).

67. Behold, I give you authority over all the enemy's power and nothing shall by any means hurt you (Luke 10:19).

68. Sickness is satanic bondage and you ought to be loosed today.

(Luke 13:16 & II Corinthians 6:2).

69. In Me is life (John 1:4).

70. I am the bread of life. I give you life (John 6:33, 35).

71. The words I speak unto you are spirit and life (John 6:63).

72. I am come that you might have life, and that you might have it more abundantly (John 10:10).

73. I am the resurrection and the life (John 11:25).

74. If you ask anything in My name, I will do it (John 14:14).

75. Faith in My name makes you strong and gives you perfect soundness (Acts 3:16).

76. I stretch forth My hand to heal (Acts 4:30).

77. I, Jesus Christ, make you whole (Acts 9:34).

78. I do good and heal all that are oppressed of the devil (Acts 10:38).

79. My power causes diseases to depart from you (Acts 19:12).

80. The law of the Spirit of life in Me has made you free from the law of sin and death (Romans 8:2).

81. The same Spirit that raised Me from the dead now lives in you and that Spirit will quicken your mortal body (Romans 8:11).

82. Your body is a member of Me (I Corinthians 6:15).

83. Your body is the temple of My Spirit and you're to glorify Me in your body (I Corinthians 6:19-20).

84) If you'll rightly discern My body which was broken for you, and judge yourself, you'll not be judged and you'll not be weak, sickly or die prematurely (I Corinthians 11:29-31).

85. I have set gifts of healing in My body (I Corinthians 12:9).

86. My life may be made manifest in your mortal flesh (II Corinthians 4:10-11).

87. I have delivered you from death, I do deliver you, and if you trust Me I will yet deliver you (II Corinthians 1:10).

88. I have given you My name and have put all things under your feet (Ephesians 1:21-22).

89. I want it to be well with you and I want you to live long on the earth. (Ephesians 6:3).

90. I have delivered you from the authority of darkness (Colossians 1:13).

91. I will deliver you from every evil work (II Timothy 4:18).

92. I tasted death for you. I destroyed the devil who had the power of death. I've delivered you from the fear of death and bondage (Hebrews 2:9, 14-15).

93. I wash your body with pure water (Hebrews 10:22; Ephesians 5:26).

94. Lift up the weak hands and the feeble knees. Don't let that which is lame be turned aside but rather let Me heal it (Hebrews 12:12-13).

95. Let the elders anoint you and pray for you in My name and I will raise you up (James 5:14-15).

96. Pray for one another and I will heal you (James 5:16).

97. By My stripes you were healed (I Peter 2:24).

98. My Divine power has given unto you all things that pertain unto life and godliness through the knowledge of Me (II Peter 1:3).

99. Whosoever will, let him come and take of the water of life freely. (Revelation 22:17).

100. Beloved, I wish above all things that you may be in health (3 John 2).

Day One

REDEEMED: SPIRIT, SOUL, AND BODY

"...Without the shedding of blood, there is no remission of sin."

Hebrews 9:22

Salvation, the gift of God to humanity, found only in Jesus the Christ. Throughout the generations, salvation has been debated, argued, resisted, received, and revered. Religions have been built upon it, wars have been fought on its behalf, nations have been founded because of it, and multitudes have entered into an eternity with God because of it. Throughout the ages, theologians have attempted to explain salvation, and as a result, various denominations, theological beliefs, and religious persuasions have become a part of our global cultures.

Many believe that salvation is simply a spiritual experience to determine your eternal fate. But is that true? Is there more? The premise of this book is to uncover for ourselves the truth regarding salvation, health, healing, wholeness, and the redemptive promises of God as they pertain to us as believers. *How* we uncover that truth is what will make the difference. This book is not based on a theological or personal opinion but strictly on the Word of God. Every chapter is supported by word studies done in the original Hebrew and Greek and interpreted with contextual clarity and concise literal and literary translation.

Lessons of Healing

The basis of salvation is the blood of Jesus Christ: In the absence of the shed blood of Jesus, there is no redemption, but *with* it, redemption becomes a reality. Remission: (Aphesis) – means to be forgiven, pardoned, and redeemed from the penalty of sin and released from bondage.

In the Old Testament, the word salvation is "Yeshuah," which is the name of Jesus and represents the character of God, the nature of God, and the heart of God. Yeshuah means deliverance, welfare, prosperity, and victory. It's essential to keep in mind that these salvation characteristics are heaven's reality, meaning these promises are relative to our life and existence on earth. In the New Testament, the original root word is "Sozo," which means to deliver from danger and destruction, keep safe and sound, heal, restore to health, and deliver from evil.

Examining both of these definitions, we can accurately conclude that salvation is total redemption for total man: spirit, soul, and body. But let's not stop there. Remember, salvation is the result of redemption by the blood, not by "word definitions." I believed that the blood that Jesus shed was the sole experience of the cross all of my life. It was not until I was on a trip in Israel and assigned to do a devotion in the Garden of Gethsemane that it dawned on me that Jesus shed His precious blood three different times, in three other locations for three different reasons. Those reasons were to provide total redemption for total man; spirit, soul, and body.

The First Shedding of Blood: The first place that Jesus shed His blood was actually in the Garden of Gethsemane. Luke 22:39-44, *"Jesus went out as usual to the Mount of Olives, and his disciples followed him. On reaching the place, he said to them, "Pray that you will not fall into temptation." He withdrew about a stone's throw beyond them, knelt, and prayed, "Father, if you are willing, take this cup from me; yet not my will, but yours be done." An angel from heaven appeared to him and strengthened him. And being in anguish, he prayed more earnestly, and his sweat was like drops of blood falling to the ground."*

Why did Jesus shed His blood in this particular location, and what was the point? The Garden was the crossroads of the redemptive plan of God for humanity. This is where the battle was won, and it all took place in the mind, will, and emotions of Jesus. The anguish of the cross and all that it represented was humanly overwhelming. An epic battle of the ages was being waged in the will of Jesus, and He not only answered it within Himself (by surrendering His will to the Father) but also paying a great price for the redemption of our souls (our mind, will, and emotions). Isaiah 53:5 says that *"But he was pierced for our transgressions, he was crushed for our iniquities; the punishment that brought us peace was on him, and by his stripes, we are healed."*

The Shedding of Blood for Healing: The second location where Jesus shed His blood was the scourging post. At the mercy of Roman soldiers (more precisely six executioners), Jesus received a minimum of 39 brutal lashes (that was Jewish law, but with the Romans, it was most likely more) with a whip made out of 7 strands of leather that had pieces of bone and lead attached to it which caused it to cut deeper into the flesh.

The point of this scourging was to bring the victim as close as possible to the end of death, without actually dying.

While drunken, half-dazed executioners, enflamed and enticed by the very powers of hell, beat the life out of Jesus, He endured the torture, the humiliation, the agony, and the shame so that by His stripes we might be healed. Isaiah 53:5, *"But he was pierced for our transgressions, he was crushed for our iniquities; the punishment that brought us peace was on him, and by his stripes, we are healed."* His willingness to suffer physically at the hands of the demonic provided the redemptive basis for our physical healing. He who was whole became broken so that we who are broken might become whole.

Redemption on the Cross: Finally, on Golgotha, hanging on a cross, the precious Lamb of God, who came to "take away the sins of the world," did exactly that. Colossians 1:19-22, "...in Jesus, all the fullness of God was pleased to dwell, and through him to reconcile to himself all things, whether on earth or in heaven, making peace by the blood of his cross. And you, who once were estranged and hostile in mind, doing evil deeds, he has now reconciled in his body of flesh by his death, to present you holy and blameless and irreproachable before him." Jesus willingly gave of

Himself to reconcile us to the Father. His sinless, perfect body hung between heaven and earth. His blood flowed, draining the life out of His earthly body so that we might have life and have it in abundance.

This chapter was intentionally written first in order to establish a theology and thus a conviction that it is _always_ the perfect will of God to heal your body. Your health, healing, and wholeness are not up for grabs or something that your intercessory efforts can purchase. You don't secure your healing by having enough people pray or by you praying long enough or hard enough. Healing is a covenant right established by the Father and purchased on your behalf by the Lord Jesus. It is secured by your faith and by your action of standing on the redemptive promises of the Word. That's what this book is all about, to inform and educate you on precisely what those promises are, giving you a firm foundation to stand on so that you don't have to walk in doubt or unbelief.

As the Word of God flows into your spirit and serves to develop your beliefs and convictions, it will become the reality of who you are and will bring about transformation in terms of the way you think, act, talk, and the perspective you have in life. It will all become relative to the will of God and the purposes of God for yourself and your family. The deposit of redemptive health is already released on the inside of you at the point of your salvation. At the point of your need, rise, and draw upon what has been invested into you. Draw out the Word of Healing, stand on the covenant promises found in the Word, and watch the manifestation of health, healing, and wholeness in your life.

Today's Confession of Healing

I am not moved by what I see, hear, or feel. I am a believer and not a doubter, and I stand today on the authority, the power, and the virtue of the Word of God in my life. I am the redeemed of God; spirit, soul, and body.

Jesus paid the total price for my peace, and as a result, I have the mind of Christ and operate in His purposes, thoughts, and intentions towards me. By the stripes of Jesus, I am healed, and I will not open the door for sickness in my thoughts, beliefs, speech, or actions.

I am saved from destruction, I am delivered from evil, I am pardoned and redeemed from the penalty of sin and its curse, and I walk in the blessing of Abraham.

Day Two

JESUS CHRIST IS LORD

"Therefore God also has highly exalted Him and given Him the name, which is above every name, that at the name of Jesus every knee should bow, of those in heaven, and of those on earth, and of those under the earth, and that every tongue should confess that Jesus Christ is Lord, to the glory of God the Father."

Philippians 2:9-11

We now come to one of the most essential and authoritative scriptures relative to walking in health and wholeness. You must know the exact place that sickness or disease has in your life and begin to walk in a kingdom mindset that will never waiver no matter what you face. Let's make this clear: sickness is *never* the will of God, and there is no place of compromise for it in the life of a believer. God does not ask you to coexist with sickness, and there is no place in the Word where God uses disease as a part of His interaction with His children. One test that I always use is what I call the "father's heart" test. I ask myself the question, "as a father, would I do that in my children's life"? If the answer is no, then I am confident that neither would my heavenly Father. He is wiser, kinder, more loving than I am, and His ways are highly exalted above mine. When my children are sick, I stand in faith and would do anything in my power to relieve them. How much greater is our God?

Lessons of Healing

You Have Dominion Over Sickness: So, where does sickness belong? It belongs under your feet. God has "highly exalted" Jesus over all, and He rules with absolute dominion and authority over heaven, on the earth, and under the earth. <u>We must understand that all sin is connected with sickness, but not all sickness is connected with sin.</u>

In other words, there are times when blatant and willful sin opens the door to sickness, but there are other times when a sickness is nothing more than a matter of living in a fallen world where you encounter viruses, diseases, etc. No matter what situation you find yourself in, sickness can never be categorized as the will or the intention of God, and Jesus is Lord over all illness, disease, and infirmity.

Why is this scripture so important? It establishes your place of authority and the right that you have as a believer to posture yourself in faith regarding the battle that you might be facing or ever will face. Jesus has been given the Name above *every* name. His name is the rank, the authority, and the ability to command. He only commands His will and His purposes over your life, and that will has already been expressed in the scripture "by His stripes, you are healed." The name of Jesus is "Jeshua," which means "Jehovah who is our salvation." We have already learned that salvation is our prosperity, deliverance, health, blessing, and protection. So what is every knee bowing to? They are bowing and giving way to the blessing of God over our lives, which is our salvation. Every knee will bow, and every tongue will confess that He is Lord. Jesus is Lord means that Jesus is the Christ, the Messiah, and the Anointed One.

Sickness, disease, infirmity, and anything else that is contrary to the will of God must give way and submit to the anointing that is in Christ Jesus, and that operates in your life as a believer. We live by the anointing, we survive by the anointing, and we *thrive* by the anointing.

God Glories in Your Health: God doesn't receive glory in your weaknesses or your infirmity. He receives glory by you being in His perfect will, and that never includes sickness. I'm not saying that you are out of God's will if you are sick, but that the sickness is out of His will, and you have the place and the authority to address it by the Word. How do you do that? Rise in faith and command it to bow and bend its knee to the authority of the anointing.

Today's Confession of Healing

I will not coexist with sickness or disease. There is no place for it in my life or my family. I am the redeemed of God, and I will not waiver in my faith or my confession that Jesus Christ is Lord over all that concerns me, to the glory of God the Father.

Sickness is never the will of God, and its existence in my body does not glorify him. I stand against sickness by the authority of the Name of Jesus, the supremacy of Jesus, and the anointing of Jesus.

I live by the anointing, I survive by the anointing, and I thrive by the anointing.

Day Three

CALL FOR THE ELDERS OF THE CHURCH

"Is anyone among you suffering? Let him pray. Is anyone cheerful? Let him sing psalms. Is anyone among you sick? Let him call for the elders of the church, and let them pray over him, anointing him with oil in the name of the Lord. And the prayer of faith will save the sick, and the Lord will raise him up. And if he has committed sins, he will be forgiven. Confess your trespasses to one another and pray for one another that you may be healed. The effective, fervent prayer of a righteous man avails much."

James 5:13-16

This is an essential scripture in our understanding of health, healing, and wholeness, and the doctrine of the local expression of the body of Christ, of which you are a part. This scripture deals explicitly with two issues that require the intervention and the faith of others. The word "suffering" is in the context of a battle that has come against you, and the source of it is discerned as demonic. This is an attack from the enemy and an affliction that originates from the realms of darkness. When you know that you are under this type of attack, it's not a time to stand alone but gather the prayer warriors together and launch a counterattack. I love that the Greek word used here for prayer describes prayer as being your *advantage.* You could restate this as: "whenever you are under attack from the enemy, gather the prayer warriors together, and rise in faith, which is your advantage."

Lessons of Healing

Call for the Elders: There are also times when you face sickness, and it becomes a battle that needs to be waged with other warriors standing with you in faith. The context is in reference to someone who has been weakened, is feeble and powerless, and the conflict has become much more significant than them. It's not the time to cower in fear or attempt to stand alone in the struggle but to rally the troops in calling for the church's elders to stand with you.

Please rest assured this is not a religious ceremony but a divine strategy of warfare. These aren't elders who are just going through the motions of prayer but are faith-filled leaders who know how to lay hold of the promises of the Word on your behalf. These elders are genuine in their faith, righteous, and possess prayer lives are potent and effective.

The Oil of Anointing: The anointing of oil is a divine strategy that represents the Holy Spirit's divine intervention. When the elders anoint with oil and invoke the name of Jesus, they are standing on the Word in authority as they pray by the authority of Jesus. It must be clear that these elders aren't gathering to beg and plead that the Lord would intervene in your life. They are standing on the Word in faith and confidence, releasing the Word with authority into your physical body. The "name" of Jesus isn't just uttering the words…"in the name of Jesus," it's the release of the authority of His name that every knee would bow and every tongue confess that He is Lord (Philippians 2:10).

Healing Is Found in Salvation: This scripture promises that the sick person will "experience salvation." If you remember, the word for healing is "sozo," and it is the same word for salvation and the born-again experience. What does that mean? Does it mean that we experience the initial work of salvation all over again? No. It means that the work of salvation in Christ is spirit, soul, *and* body. Your faith and that of the elders lay ahold of the promise that is already yours. The provision is no different; it is the work that has already been accomplished in you. We just tapped into one of the essential principles and laws of health and healing.

Everything that you need to walk in divine health is already on the inside of you. It has already been accomplished and made fully available to you in your salvation. The response of the Lord is to "raise you."

What does that mean? It means to "stir you up." Stir what up? He's stirring up the work of redemption that has already been accomplished on the inside of you. So, where does healing originate? It originates from the accomplished work of Jesus through redemption and has been deposited on the inside of you. The contact and point of agreement that the elders are making is the stirring up of your faith and the laying ahold of the provision that is already yours by redemption.

Today's Confession of Healing

I will not walk alone. In faith, I join hands with my brothers and sisters who stand with me in laying hold of the provision of my salvation. God's perfect will for me is redemptive; spirit, soul, and body.

I rise in the advantage that I have in declaring and proclaiming God's Word over my life. The enemy is defeated, and I engage the divine strategy of unified faith and prayer against all of his lies and ploys. I am the healed of God. I stir up the gift and the provision of healing that has already been deposited in my spirit by making Jesus the Lord of my life.

Day Four

THIS IS THE CONFIDENCE

"Now this is the confidence that we have in Him, that if we ask anything according to His will, He hears us. And if we know that He hears us, whatever we ask, we know that we have the petitions that we have asked of Him."

1 John 5:14-15

Much of this book has been about building theology to understand that God's will to heal *all* sickness and disease is *always* His will. There is a prevalent mindset within specific sectors of the Body of Christ that God uses sickness to bring about His will in your life and that He may choose *not* to heal you depending on what His will may be in that particular circumstance. Sickness cannot be validated in the Word of God as <u>ever</u> being the will of God in *any* situation.

I have seen many people use their personal experiences of somebody who was a godly person and was not healed as validation of this line of thought. To use anything other than the Word of God is to make the theology of healing subjective, and God's Word will not be subjected to humanity's experiences. To do so would make the Word of God relative. His Word is accurate and the final authority. So, what does the Word say about His will, and how do we pray in the will of God?

Lessons of Faith

Praying in the Will of God: Whenever you pray in the will of God, you can always pray with confidence. Not just in terms of knowing the will of God, but *how* you pray and *how* you talk. When you know the will of God, you don't have to waiver from understanding the truth of His Word. To pray with confidence is to pray without any sense of ambiguity; it is to pray with cheerful courage and assurance that God is for you and never against you. God desires His will to come to fruition, and He will continually work to align circumstances in your life to His perfect will.

Walking in Holy Confidence: The scripture for today tells us that we can have confidence that comes from knowing His will and that we can rise in faith and possess the will of God even before it comes into full manifestation. That's the power of faith. The scripture says that it is "*a confidence which we have before Him.*" That word means that it's our "advantage."

The advantage that we have of knowing that God watches over His Word to perform it. This level of prayer is not "asking" God to do something and just hoping that He will. This is a level of authority and faith that comes into alignment with God's revealed will by His Word and comes into agreement with what He has already decreed and declared. This is a level of "ask" that requires circumstances outside of God's will (sickness and disease) to come into submission to the will of God.

So, do you have to "determine" what the will of God is in every single situation and then align yourself with what you believe to be the will of God? There are specific issues that God has already addressed in His Word and divine principles by which we live that have established God's predetermined will. The word "will" is the Greek word "Thelema," and it means the "predetermined purposes of God to bless mankind through Christ, the inclination of God, the desires and the choice of God." Do sickness and disease bless humanity? Does poverty bless humanity? Does sin bless humanity? Anything contrary to the blessing of God as outlined in His word is *never* the will of God for your life.

God's Word is God's Will: You can address any situation in your life, line it up with what the Word says about it, what the Word says about you, and then begin to pray the Word over that situation. God's Word is His will, and whenever you pray the Word of God, you *are* praying the will of God and can pray with utmost confidence and authority. You don't have to ask God to do something that He has already stated is His will. You declare the Word into and over any situation, knowing that you are expressing the will of the Father. When you pray (say and decree) at that level, this scripture assures us that He hears or "attends to" the very thing that you are declaring. When you pray like that, you will have the petitions that you asked of Him.

Today's Confession of Healing

God's Word is God's will, and I refuse to settle for anything less than His perfect choice for my life and my family. I will not be moved by anything less than what God declares in His Word over me.

I rise with confidence in knowing that God's perfect plan for my life is to bless me and His choice and desire is that I would walk and live in the fulfillment of all His redemptive purposes over me.

I stand in faith with cheerful confidence and in the advantage of knowing that God watches over His Word to perform it in my life.

Day Five

UNDER HIS WINGS

"Surely He shall deliver you from the snare of the fowler and from the perilous pestilence. He shall cover you with His feathers, and under His wings, you shall take refuge; His truth shall be your shield and buckler.
You shall not be afraid of the terror by night, or of the arrow that flies by day, or of the pestilence that walks in darkness, or of the destruction that lays waste at noonday."

Psalm 91:3-6

To read this scripture at face value is to realize that the Father's heart of God towards His children is one of protection, security, and safety from the disasters that life can bring. However, looking closer and studying this, we quickly realize that this scripture explicitly refers to the healing virtue of the Lord being released in your life.

God's heart is never to use any of the enemy's weapons of mass destruction to teach you His will or to shape your life in any way. God doesn't have to stoop to those ugly ploys to teach you His will and purposes; it's the job of the Holy Spirit to lead you and guide you into all truth. God's heart is to rescue you and to save you from the calamity that the enemy would bring against you.

In this text, God reveals that when you are entangled and

33

trapped by sickness. His will is to bring you into a safe and healthy place. The term "perilous pestilence" means to be engulfed and ruined by disease and plague, which is the very thing that He promised the children of Israel He would "not allow to be put upon them" and "would deliver them from if only they would follow" after Him. If it's not His desire, will, or intention for the children of Israel, why would He want that for you? He does not.

Lessons of Faith

Covered by God: He longs to cover and protect you like an eagle protects her young. Eagles are a symbol of strength, courage, freedom, and immortality. They are called the "lions of the sky." In Deuteronomy 32:11-13, the Lord is described as an "*eagle that hovers over its young.*" This is the same word used in Genesis 1:2, that the "*Spirit of God hovered over the deep.*" Like an eagle, God was preparing a nest to protect humanity.

That's His heart towards you. Eagles build their nests high and away from the terror of predators. They are incredibly territorial, protecting the nest from other eagles, predators, or intruders. Whenever the eaglets are young and most at risk to the attack from enemies, that's when the mother and father eagle are most on alert. They watch over their brood with a careful eye and are ready to protect at the slightest sign of danger. When it comes to protecting their children, they are incredibly jealous and become fierce in the face of danger. That's precisely what God means when He says that

"I will cover you with My feathers and under my wings, you will find refuge" (protection, confidence, and hope).

Healing in His Wings: He promises that *"under His wings, you will find protection."* What are those wings? They are "wings of healing." Malachi 4:2, *"But for you who fear my name, the sun of righteousness will rise with healing in its wings..."* These healing wings are referenced in Matthew 9:20-22 when the woman with the issue of blood touched the "hem of the garment" that Jesus was wearing. She touched the "tzitzit" or the tassels on the edge of the tallit (prayer garment) that Jesus had on.

These were considered the wings of healing and represented the authority that a man had from following and being obedient to the Word of the Lord. Numbers 15:37-41, *"The Lord said to Moses, 'Speak to the Israelites and say to them: Throughout the generations to come, you are to make tassels on the corners of one's garments, with a blue cord on each tassel. You will have these tassels to look at and so will remember all the commands of the Lord, that you may obey them and not prostitute yourselves by going after the lusts of your hearts and eyes. Then you will remember to obey all My commands and will be consecrated to your God. I am the Lord your God."*

That precious woman touched the authority that Jesus walked in because of His complete surrender to the Lord. That's the place that God wants to bring you. As you surrender to His will and His Word, He will cover you with His authority and His healing touch.

The realization of your healing is under the authority of the Word over your life.

The Shield of Faith: God also promises that during the heat of the battle, when the enemy is hammering you with fear and dread and the lies of disease, He will surround you with His shield. This is not just any ordinary shield. The shields described in the Psalms are those that extend the entire length of the body. It had a flexibility that would cover any unprotected part of the body. It was designed to quench any fiery arrows that would be launched at them. This is the shield of faith; your conviction that God's word over you is not debatable and will not be denied. God covers you with His healing virtue, and your faith lays ahold of it and appropriates it in your particular situation.

Today's Confession of Healing

My life is not up for grabs, and the protective heart of God secures me. I hide under His wings of healing, and in His protective care, the evil one cannot touch me. I am covered and protected by the Word, and by the authority of the Word, I am healed, healthy, and happy. The Word is my shield and my refuge; I will not surrender to or listen to the lies of terror and dread. I hear the voice of the Good Shepherd, and His voice only will I follow.

Day Six

REDEEMED FROM THE CURSE OF THE LAW

"Christ has redeemed us from the curse of the law, having become a curse for us (for it is written, "Cursed is everyone who hangs on a tree that the blessing of Abraham might come upon the Gentiles in Christ Jesus, that we might receive the promise of the Spirit through faith."

Galatians 3:13-14

As a born-again believer, there are two essential issues that we must understand. Firstly, you must know what the "curse of the law" is. That understanding enables you to understand precisely what you have been redeemed. Secondly, you need to know and understand the "blessing of Abraham" to embrace the promises that are yours. In Christ, we are the redeemed of God, and there are specific covenants and redemptive promises that belong to you because of who you are in Christ. It's your inheritance.

I've never heard of a single person who knew they had an inheritance coming and yet, chose <u>not</u> to be informed of what they were inheriting. Quite the contrary, if you know that you will inherit something of great value, you will want to be fully informed and act on whatever you need to do to secure your inheritance. So it is with redemption and the covenant promise. You need to be fully informed and walk in faith to lay hold of what belongs to you.

Lessons of Faith

The Price has been Paid: I am the redeemed of God. The price has been paid, and my life has been fully recovered from the power of the enemy. He has no claim against me: spirit, soul, or body. Anything that the enemy attempts to perpetrate against me is based on a lie. The enemy has no right, no authority, and no basis for ensnaring or captivating God's people. All of his activities are illegal, based on a lie, and must be judged as such.

Redeemed from the Curse: From what exactly have we been redeemed? The curse of the law is the result of not walking in obedience to the Word of God. The Word is our covering and our protection. It is the source of our faith and the basis of the blessing. The result of not being grounded in the Word and not living under the Word covering is that you are exposed to the enemy's onslaught. The curse defines the penalty for walking in disobedience: sickness, disease, poverty, lack, pain, suffering, and plagues. None of these are the will or desire of God upon His people.

In Christ, you are redeemed and protected from all of those curses. Our covenant relationship with Him redeems us from and removes all the power of sickness and disease. Because of Jesus, we no longer have to live under the penalty of poverty or lack, suffering, pain, or plagues. Will the enemy attempt to put these things upon you? Absolutely. If you do not know that you have "redemptive rights," you will never stand up in faith against the attack of the enemy, and he will do everything in his power to captivate you and hold you hostage.

What About the Blessing? We have established that we do not have to tolerate any of the law's curses and that we should stand against them in faith, but what about the blessing? It's interesting to me that in today's scripture reading, Paul points out that two specific covenant benefits resulted from the sacrifice that Jesus made on our behalf. Firstly, he says that we are now postured to receive and walk in the same blessing that God gave to Abraham, and secondly, we would receive the promise of the Spirit through faith. That's a double dose of favor, blessing, and promise.

The blessing of Abraham is found in Deuteronomy 28. This is a promise given to Abraham and passed on to Israel's children if they would continue to serve the Lord, walk in faith and obedience, and follow after God with a whole heart. These are the blessings that will come upon us, overtake us, and are now available to us because of Christ:

- You will be blessed no matter where you live, city, or country.
- Your children will be blessed.
- Your enemies will be defeated before you.
- Your storehouses will be blessed and overflowing.

- All that you put your hand to will be blessed.
- Your physical body will be blessed.
- You will be granted plenty of goods.
- You shall be a lender and not a borrower.
- You will be the head and not the tail.
- You will be above only and not beneath.

That's the definition of the Christian life. That's the life that God intended for His children to live, and by faith, that's the description of the perfect will of God. To live that life, you must stand and contend for all that is yours in Christ Jesus. The enemy did everything he could to distract Israel from living this kind of life. He tempted them with other ways of doing life; he engaged them in religion's lies, causing their faith to become doubt and unbelief. Few too many today believe that God wants us to live lives like this, and few dare to posture themselves in faith and make these kinds of declarations, which is why this book is so important.

All of the curses result from the law of sin and death, but there is a more significant law that transcends that, and it's the law of life found in Christ Jesus. Several years ago, I discovered a literal definition of the word "blessed" drawn from this text. Blessed: *"anointed to win, empowered to prosper, impossible to curse,"* may that be true in your life today.

Today's Confession of Healing

I am free; I am blessed; I am what the Word says I am. I walk in the blessing of Abraham that I have in Christ. By the blood of Jesus, I rise in faith and resist all of the curses of the law.

I am free from the law of sin and death. I now live according to the law of life that is in Christ Jesus. I am blessed in the city and the country; my children are blessed, my storehouse is blessed and overflowing, all that I put my hand to is blessed; I am the head and not the tail.

I am above only and not beneath; I am a lender and not a borrower. I am anointed to win, empowered to prosper, impossible to curse.

Day Seven

NOW FAITH

"Now, faith is the substance of things hoped for, the evidence of things not seen. By it, the elders obtained a good testimony. By faith, we understand that the worlds were framed by the Word of God so that the things which are seen were not made of visible things."

Hebrews 11:1-3

What moves the heart of God? Coming into agreement and alignment with His Word, His will, and His plans and purposes over your life. The entire Kingdom of God and all that concerns it is built upon the law of God and is governed by the principles of that law. Of the two kingdoms, God's kingdom is established upon the law of life in Christ Jesus and is governed by faith principles. That level of faith comes by hearing the Word of God and being shaped, fashioned, and formed by the Word.

To walk in faith is to think the Word, to speak the Word, to act on the Word, and to be motivated by the Word of God in every circumstance of your life. Your faith is your conviction. The definition of conviction is "a firmly held belief and opinion: view, thought, persuasion, position, and stance." In other words, your "kingdom faith" is your conviction that God's Word is truth and is the ultimate and final authority in your life and in any circumstance that you might face. It's a "*now*" faith and is dependent upon your submission to the dictates, standards, and principles of the Word in your life, no matter what it looks like, feels like, or what you might hear or think.

Lessons of Faith

The Substance of Faith: Your faith is the very substance upon which you establish your expectations. The word "substance" is literally to "set in place by the authority that you have in the Word of God. It means to become steadfast, resolute, and confident. That confidence paves the way for your expectations. Has somebody that you trust ever made a promise to you? Based on your relational trust, you have every confidence that they will do what they say, and you live your life with expectancy until that promise is fulfilled. It doesn't matter that others may tell you that it's not going to happen, or if it takes longer than you initially expected, you "know" that person, and no matter what it looks like or what you hear, you don't budge from your confidence and your expectancy.

That's how this works. You build confidence based upon a relationship with the Lord through His Word, and you begin to trust that what He has said concerning you will come to past, no matter what. That relational trust becomes your confident expectancy and your conviction. That's all the evidence you need, that's all the conviction you need. God's Word is true no matter what you are facing, and now you can face it with absolute certainty, confidence, and expectancy; that's faith.

Framed by the Word: The very world itself was "framed" by the Word of God. That means that all of the world's elements are subject to the authority of the Word, and it has the final say. Throughout the Bible, we find that the world's natural elements had to submit to the Word's authority. Now you know why the Red Sea had to part, why the sun had to stand still, why the waves and weather had to submit to the authority of Jesus, and why the water itself had to hold him up. There are recorded instances of people speaking to tornadoes and watching them move in another direction or completely dissipate. What's the lesson here? The realm of the natural does not dictate your life. We are a supernatural people and live by a higher authority that is the ultimate word over the natural world, including sickness and disease.

Today's Confession of Faith

I am a person of great faith. I walk by faith, I talk by faith, and I live by faith. The just shall live by faith, and I have been given the measure of faith.

The increase of my faith comes from my investment of the Word of God into my spirit. I live by the law of life that is in Christ Jesus and have been set free from the law of sin and death.

I am not moved by what I see, what I hear, or even what I think. I stand on the final authority of the Word of God over my life, and I command my body to supernaturally align itself with the Word of health, healing, and wholeness.

Day Eight

POWER OF THE TONGUE

"A man's stomach shall be satisfied from the fruit of his mouth; from the produce of his lips, he shall be filled. Death and life are in the power of the tongue, and those who love it will eat its fruit."

Proverbs 18:20-21

How important are the words that come out of your mouth? Once again, this is an issue of great debate within the Body of Christ. Specific camps are almost legalistic in terms of what you say, and others practically mock those who believe in the power of words, calling them the "name it and claim it" crowd. As always, we go back to the authority and the voice of the Word of God. According to the scripture reading today, the words you speak are important, and actually, your very life could depend on them.

The word "stomach" isn't referring to the organ that exists within your abdomen. It means your physical body and your mental faculties. In other words, both your physical body *and* mind are affected by the words you use. It's by the fruit of your mouth that your physical body is satisfied or enriched and fulfilled. It means to live in health and wholeness with nothing lacking and nothing missing. The fruit of your mouth is the actual "fruitfulness" that you will experience due to the words of action that you declare.

Remember, whenever you speak and declare the Word of God, you are proclaiming the will of God.

Lessons of Faith

The Weapon of Your Words: In the context of this scripture, the words that come out of your mouth can be used as a weapon. By your words, you can reinforce the will of God and break and shatter into pieces (pa-ah) the plans and the obstacles of the enemy that have arisen against you. Your words are strong and productive. Words are seeds and inside of every seed is a harvest. Words released in faith and authority find their place, take root, and produce the crop they intended.

Your faith is the conviction that God's Word is confirmed; your mouth is the releasing agent that connects your faith to the need. A good analogy of this is a doctor giving a shot. There is a healing antibiotic within the cylinder, and there is a need within the physical body. The needle that's attached to the cylinder becomes the agent that punctures the skin as it is inserted into the body, and through it, the antibiotic is released. So it is with faith and your words.

There is a strong anointing and conviction on the inside of you, and there is an evident need in your life. Your words become the needle that releases the conviction and faith into the situation, declaring the will of God over it without wavering. Your words release life, healing, and blessing.

Life and Death: Let's take a look at this issue of death and life. In both of these instances, we will be wise to visit the original language to gain a greater sense of clarity and understanding. The Hebrew word for death is "Muth," and it means to die prematurely. Does that mean that people have died before their time because of their words? The Bible says in Proverbs 23:7 that "*as a man thinks in his heart, so is he.*" I have heard people declaring ungodly things over their lives, and thus, inadvertently opening the door and giving the enemy permission to have his way over them.

Becoming God-Inside Minded: The good news is that when you become God-inside minded and your words begin to reflect the will of God, the result is life. Again, let's examine the original language to glean an accurate understanding. The term used here is "chayah," which means prosperity, restoration, and quickened from sickness, and to be healthy.

While that is exciting, I have to point out that it is the same word found in Genesis 2:7, when God breathed "life" into Adam. "*And the LORD God formed man of the dust of the ground, and breathed into his nostrils the breath of life, and man became a living being.*" This is the first recorded instance of CPR. God breathed His very life into that which had no life, and Adam became the first living being. In today's scripture, we are told that we have that same power and authority. Our words release that power into whatever situation we might be facing.

Releasing the Breath of God: Do you have a suffering or dying situation and need life? Do what God did, release life into it. He did it with His very breath, and when you use the words of your mouth, you are releasing the breath of the Spirit of God that's inside of you into that situation, and the result is life. Use your words in faith, use them in authority being careful not to let idle and ungodly words come out of your mouth.

In particular, be aware of any words that work against the will of God in your life in terms of health and healing. I often hear people refer to sickness in terms of ownership. "My arthritis is acting up again." It's not your arthritis. It belongs to the devil; it's not the will of God for your life, so stop embracing it and stop owning it. I also hear people confess what's physically wrong with them without ever making their corresponding confession of faith or declaring what God says about their situation. It looks like this, "how are you feeling today?" "I'm under the weather." Never leave it at that.

Always say what God says about you, "I'm under the weather, but according to the Word of God, I am healed, in Jesus' Name." When you do that, you just spoke life and released the very breath of God over your physical body. The result is health, healing, and wholeness, and that is the will of God. You will be fruitful from the life that is released from your words and language.

Today's Confession of Faith

My words are powerful; my words are a weapon that can defeat the enemy's plans and purposes over my life when used in faith and godly authority.

By my words, faith is released, so I choose today to align my words with what God says and only what God says. I will not allow idle or ungodly words to come out of my mouth, and I will never let my words be used for destructive purposes.

I will only use my words to build up and encourage others and release the prosperity, the blessing, health, and restoration of the Word. I walk by faith; I think by faith, I live by faith, and I talk by faith.

Day Nine

TAKE THIS BREAD

"For I received from the Lord what I also passed on to you: The Lord Jesus, on the night he was betrayed, took bread, and when he had given thanks, he broke it and said, "This is my body, which is for you; do this in remembrance of me." In the same way, after supper, he took the cup, saying, "This cup is the new covenant in my blood; do this, whenever you drink it, in remembrance of me." For whenever you eat this bread and drink this cup, you proclaim the Lord's death until he comes."

I Corinthians 11:23-26

One of the most significant misunderstandings in the Body of Christ is communion. In many circles, it has been relegated to nothing more than a religious observance held on a weekly or monthly basis, mainly becoming symbolic with little or no biblical significance. The truth is that communion is one of the most powerful spiritual weapons that the church has been given.

When you begin to walk in a complete understanding of its power and significance, you will unlock the potential and the purpose of the elements of communion in your life. There is much symbolism found in the elements of communion, beginning with the bread. The original root word for bread is "airo." This is typical bread used in Israel for the celebration of Passover as well as other gatherings. It is unleavened bread about the width of your thumb and the size of a platter. What's interesting is that the word itself means to "be lifted," "to take upon oneself and to bear a burden," to "take from among the living, either by a natural death or by violence." Little did the Jewish people know that all of the years of partaking in Passover, they were receiving that which represented the Lord Jesus being lifted and hung on a cross. Jesus took that bread and "broke" it. In Jesus, nothing was broken, nothing was missing, nothing was empty.

He was whole and complete but chose to become broken for our sake and on our behalf so that we who were broken might become whole. It is in His brokenness that the curse has been reversed. When He broke the bread, He declared that His body (soma) was being broken. Let's go back to discover the original word. It's the word "Sozo" and is also the original word for salvation. It means delivered from suffering and disease, to make well, heal and restore, and save from destruction and judgment.

Lessons of Faith

Communion is a Spiritual Weapon: Jesus took the bread. He broke it, declaring that it represented Himself. He then made a striking statement that we often confuse and misinterpret in the church today. When He uttered the words, "do this in remembrance of me," He was equipping us with one of the most powerful spiritual weapons that we have in our arsenal against sickness and disease. The word remembrance is not a casual calling to mind or having a sense of memory that evokes emotions. This is a powerful term that means so much more.

The Greek word is "anamimnḗskō," and it means to "lay hold of" with authority, "to consider well and remind yourself and to weigh well" precisely what you are doing. It also means to admonish. What are you doing? You are partaking of the broken body of Jesus that represents that we are the healed of God. Whenever you receive the bread's element (the broken body of Christ), you are to make your corresponding confession of what that means; by the stripes of Jesus, I am healed. Jesus paid the redemptive price so that you could walk in healing and wholeness. It is by your "remembrance," (your faith and your confession), that you lay hold of that promise and enforce it in your life.

The Power of the Cup: After that, He took the "cup," and made another proclamation. During the Passover celebration, four specific cups were used. The cup that Jesus held up "after supper" would have been the third cup or the cup of redemption or blessing. Jesus knew exactly what He was doing. Throughout Hebrew scripture, cups represent judgment, fury, and wrath. However, David lifted the cup in Psalm 116:13 and referred to it as the *"cup of salvation."* Thus, cups are biblically known as cups of wrath and redemption, judgment, and blessing. All of that is found in the cup that Jesus lifted, filled with His precious blood.

However, this cup's difference is that it would become the cup of the new covenant and be fulfilled by the Lamb of God Himself. Jesus is the *"Lamb of God that takes away the sin of the world,"* John 1:29. The Greek word for cup is "pino" and means to receive into your soul that refreshes, strengthens, and nourishes unto eternal life. Your redemption is based solely on the provision that Jesus made on your behalf. Communion is laying ahold of those promises in faith and embracing that which Jesus accomplished for you.

Your Word of Confession: The power of this scripture is found in your proclamation. As often as you partake of the table of the Lord, you proclaim His death. Your proclamation is your confession. When you receive the broken body of the Lord, make your corresponding confession of health, healing, and wholeness. "By the stripes of Jesus, I am healed, and I stand on the provision of redemption and receive into my body the healing virtue of His brokenness." When you receive the shed blood of Jesus as represented by the cup of redemption, make your corresponding confession of redemption, peace, forgiveness, and wholeness. "By the blood of Jesus, I am the redeemed of God. I lay hold of life, blessing, provision, forgiveness, and all of the redemptive promises that are mine in Christ."

Don't allow communion to become something that is merely a religious observation or ceremony, but life-giving, life-changing, and life-releasing every single time that you receive it. It is also essential to remember that communion doesn't have to be received only at church or in a corporate setting. You can and should receive it at home, particularly whenever you or your family members face sickness or disease.

I will take this opportunity to remind you that communion doesn't necessarily have to be the particular types of elements you use in your church setting. You can use the regular bread that you have in your home and grape juice, Kool-Aid, etc.; it's _what_ those elements represent and not the actual elements themselves that matter.

Today's Confession of Faith

As I receive this bread, I lay hold of the brokenness of Christ and the sacrifice that He made on my behalf. I came to the cross as a broken person, but today I receive wholeness and health from His brokenness. Jesus bore my burden and redeemed me from the curse of the law, and today I make my proclamation of faith that I am what God says I am.

As I receive the blood, I receive forgiveness, cleansing, and the Word's supernatural provision and make my proclamation of faith that the enemy cannot touch me. He is a defeated foe, and I am walking in divine favor and wholeness; spirit, soul, and body.

Day Ten

BY HIS STRIPES

"But he was wounded for our transgressions; he was bruised for our iniquities: the chastisement of our peace was upon him, and with his stripes, we are healed."

Isaiah 53:4

Health, healing, and wholeness are never decided upon by God on a situation-by-situation basis. In other words, we don't come to God whenever we need healing, and then He decides at that moment whether to grant you healing or not. It's not a coin-toss, and your health is not up for grabs. Health and wholeness are the revealed and established will of God for your life, and it is a matter of redemptive covenant. It's ALREADY been decided, and the price has been paid on your behalf.

Nowhere in the Word is this process laid out more clearly than Isaiah 53:5. He who was perfect and whole became weak, diseased, and afflicted so that we who were weak, diseased, and afflicted might be made perfect and complete. Isaiah prophetically reveals the price that Jesus would pay on our behalf. He was "wounded" (chalah), which means to become weak, sick, and diseased.

He allowed sickness to invade His body and became polluted, defiled and desecrated to establish a covenant of redemption.

As we walk through this scripture, it's essential to note several specific points of consideration. Jesus was wounded, bruised, chastised, and beaten on our behalf. He paid a high price so that you and I would be free from the tormenting lies and attacks of the enemy.

Lessons of Faith

Wounded: He was wounded for our transgression. Transgression is the Hebrew word "pasha," which means rebellion. A life of rebellion is the picture of our life before a relationship with Christ. However, it must be noted that rebellion is also a gateway through which disease finds an entrance. We must guard the gates of our lives and remain submitted to God's will, not allowing a heart or attitude of rebellion to take root, thereby opening the door to sin, sickness, and disease.

Bruised: Jesus was bruised (crushed) and broken for our iniquities. The word iniquity (Ava) means to be bent, twisted, and distorted. In other words, God's original plan and intention as revealed in the Garden of Eden was distorted by Adam's sin, thus opening the door and twisting and subverting God's plan for humanity, which was to walk in perfect health and wholeness. His chastisement (yacar) was the Father bringing correction to that which had been perverted because of sin's entry. The result was peace.

Chastised: He was chastised for our peace (shalom). This one word sums up the entirety of the covenant of salvation. The shalom of God is completeness, physical soundness, safety, welfare, health, and prosperity (nothing broken, nothing missing). What a powerful covenant from a loving, caring, kind-hearted Father. What was being corrected by the chastisement of Jesus? Eden's covenant plan and peace were restored by the sacrifices of Jesus, who willingly gave Himself to restore God's original plan of peace for you and me.

By His Stripes: Finally, Isaiah indicates that Jesus would receive stripes upon His body to secure our health and healing, and that's precisely what He did. The Hebrew word for stripes is "chabbuwrah" and means stripes, wounds, bruises, and blows. However, I want to bring your attention to the root word, which is "chabar." Chabar means to unite, be joined, and bound together.

Why is that important? It's important because of what was accomplished by the stripes of Jesus, our healing. In Exodus 15, God describes Himself as "Jehovah-Rapha," which is the same word for healing in this verse. So, by the stripes of Jesus, we are declared the "healed" of God. In other words, by the sacrifice of Jesus, the perversion is reversed, and we are divinely and redemptively united to God and can declare with confidence that we are now, precisely what God is; healthy and whole and walking in divine favor.

Today's Confession of Healing

Thank You, Lord, that it has already been decided at Calvary that I am healed, healthy, and whole. I don't have to repeatedly ask you to do what you have already completed on my behalf.

I walk in the covenant of redemption, which includes my physical healing, and that which was distorted in my life is now restored to your original intention. My covenant is one of peace, and I walk in completeness, physical health, safety, mental stability, and prosperity.

Day Eleven

FEAR NOT

"Do not fear, for I am with you; do not be dismayed; for I am your God: I will strengthen you, and I will help you. I will uphold you with the right hand of my righteousness."

Isaiah 41:10

This is a powerful word to stand on whenever you are facing any kind of sickness or disease. This scripture would be easy to overlook and could simply be read as an "encouraging devotional scripture." Still, when you begin to break it down, it's a powerful word in terms of warfare against anything that is ravaging your life or your physical body.

In this scripture, the Lord Himself gives clear directives of how to posture yourself in faith and confidence when walking through trials or tribulations. The very first instructional admonishments are "do not become afraid and do not become dismayed." The word afraid "yare" means to become dreadful of whatever you are facing and to allow the situation to cause you to become terrified. When the Lord says not to become dismayed, that word means not setting your gaze upon whatever is coming against you.

Lessons of Faith

Forget Not the Benefits: So, I have a choice to make; I can either become ensnared or captivated by the sickness that I am facing, or I can choose to set my eyes on the promises of God that He declares over me. What are those promises? They are also outlined in this verse. God addresses the issues you face and makes a strong declaration when He says: "Don't forget that I am Elohiym. I am the one true ruler and judge; I am the one, true God".

Change What You're Looking At: He begins with a declaration of Himself over you and then reveals precisely what He is going to do on your behalf. His first promise is that He will strengthen you, "amats." God says, "I will make you strong and alert; I will make you brave, bold, and solid. I will secure you and give you an obstinate determination. I will confirm you and give you a sense of superiority over what you might be facing." You can't do that when you have your eyes set on the size and the strength of your mountain. You must decide to get your eyes off of the issue and onto the One who is all that you need. God promises to support you and hold fast to you. His amazing promise is that He will literally seize you and hold fast to you.

Upheld By God: He goes on to say that "I will uphold you with the "right" hand of my salvation:" "tsedeq" – which means deliverance, victory, and prosperity as established by the law of God. That means "normality according to the purposes and intentions of God as outlined in His Word". It's important to remember that what is negatively affecting your physical body is illegal according to the Word of God and has no right to be in your body. God's will and God's purpose for you, as defined in this scripture, is His deliverance, His victory, and His prosperity.

Today's Confession of Healing

No matter what I am facing, I will not give in to the lying spirit of fear. I do not have to be terrified of what I hear or even what I see because God has me covered: spirit, soul, and body.

I chose to set my eyes on my Healer, and I will not become distracted by the circumstances that are at hand. I am strong, I am determined, and I am walking in the truth of deliverance, victory, and divine prosperity according to the Word of the Lord over my family and myself.

Day Twelve

SUPERNATURAL RESTORATION

"For I will restore health unto you, and I will heal you of your wound, says the Lord; because they called you an outcast, saying this is Zion, whom no man seeks after."

Jeremiah 30:17

The plans and the purposes of God are always about restoration. All that God is doing in His kingdom is ultimately about restoring His divine plans as established in His original creation. The original "God-design" of man was one of health, blessing, and prosperity. The enemy has consistently been attempting to erode God's purposes and causing God's people to believe a lie that they are less than what He intended them to become. God is establishing a people walking in power, authority, and the truth of the Word; YOU are one of those people.

In this scripture, we find another promise of the Lord regarding your divine health and healing. It's important to note that God is not only interested in your healing but in taking you to the next level of health; that's where He wants you to live. You are not designed nor destined to walk and live a life of sickness, but one of wholeness and health.

No matter what religion or secular society may tell you, God's plan for you is always health and never sickness.

Lessons of Faith

Supernaturally Restored: The Hebrew concept of restoration is to be "drawn you up to another level of life and understanding." God is longing to draw you to Himself and establish an understanding of His purposes that you would walk in throughout your life and would be able to draw upon, especially when you are facing a battle of sickness. The word "restore" literally means to "stir up" the gift of life and healing that is already inside you by salvation.

God's redemptive plans established His healing purposes and plans in you and for you, but it doesn't stop there. God declares in this scripture that He wants to give you a long, healthy, and prosperous life. The Father heart of God and the nature of God towards you are revealed in this scripture. That becomes your declaration and your place of faith as you stand on the authority of the Word over your life and family.

The God Who Heals: God is a God of healing, and His nature and character are always that of healing. As revealed in this scripture, one of God's names is Jehovah-Rapha, the "God of health and healing." The healing virtue of God is not only relative to the physical but to the emotional as well. The word Rapha declares that God "longs to bring health into our lives" but is also the "Healer of our distresses as well," particularly the distress that is a result of physical sickness attacking our bodies. In this scripture, He declares Himself to be the "Great Physician."

Living in Abundance, Blessing, and Health: He is the Healer of our "wounds," which speaks of the blows and the attacks of the enemy against us, as well as the effects of being in the world. Whenever you have been defeated by just "being in the world" and have become distressed and discouraged, God says that He longs to heal you of that sense of defeat and restore you to a place of life, wholeness, and victory. The Father does not want you to live under the heavy hand of failure or the scourge of the enemy. He longs for you to live in the abundance of life, blessing, and health. Thus saith the Lord.

Today's Confession of Healing

I rise today in faith and the strength of the Word. I declare over my body that I am what God says I am. God's plan and purpose for me are that I walk in divine health, healing and wholeness.

I am not designed to live in sickness. God's redemptive plan establishes the blessing of healing in my life, and I receive it NOW by faith. By faith, I stir up the gift of life, health, and healing in my body and over my family. I will not accept anything less than that which Jesus paid for on Calvary.

Day Thirteen

THE SPIRIT OF THE LORD IS UPON ME

"And He was handed the book of the prophet Isaiah. And when He had opened the book, He found the place where it was written: "The Spirit of the LORD is upon Me, Because He has anointed Me To preach the gospel to the poor; He has sent Me to heal the brokenhearted, To proclaim liberty to the captives And recovery of sight to the blind, To set at liberty those who are oppressed; To proclaim the acceptable year of the LORD."

Luke 4:17-19

Freedom. It is the will, purpose, and plan of God. It's why Jesus came and gave His life. Salvation is not just about eternal redemption, but life here on the earth as well. To understand the power of this scripture, it becomes essential that we do a word study to discern salvation in terms of God's will for believers on the earth.

As I unpack the definition of salvation, remember that none of the things described in this scripture include issues in heaven, only those here on the earth. That means that one of the primary purposes of salvation is relative to our existence on earth. The Greek word for salvation is "Soteria," which implies welfare, prosperity, deliverance, and safety. The root word is "Sozo," and it means saving, healing, preserving, and delivering. You will notice that salvation benefits relate to who we are: spirit, soul, and body. Sozo is total salvation for total man.

Lessons of Healing

Living in Revelation: Why is it essential that we understand the definition of these words? Because in this scripture, we discover God's will for those who follow Him. God's intention is found in the Gospel, or the Good News of God, the Bible. Understanding this, we quickly discover that it is not God's will for you to live your life brokenhearted or as a captive to the bondages and lies of the enemy, but to walk in revelation, liberty, and in the favor of the Lord.

God actually "anointed" Jesus to establish that message through His kingdom on the earth. It's equally vital that we understand the anointing. All that Jesus did in establishing the kingdom of God by the anointing, we are also anointed to do as we bring expansion to the kingdom. The anointing of God is the "supernatural enablement of God that exceeds your natural capacities." Jesus never operated on the earth within the context of his divinity but as the "son of man" who was anointed by God. He lived His life as a sinless, perfect man who lived by the enabling of the Holy Spirit. The good news is that it's also available to us today.

Bringing the Will of God into Reality: We live in a world that has been captivated and trapped by the lies of sin. Everywhere you turn, you see the effects of evil as it manifests itself in sickness, disease, and lives that are ravaged by the endless onslaught of the plans of the enemy. Religion cannot respond to this attack.

Only God's plans and purposes as carried out through His church can bring the will of God into reality. As believers, we are the "proclaimers" of this good news, and through our lives, we become vessels through which God can "set the captive free." God's will is divine restoration in every arena of our lives: spirit, soul, and body. To be "blinded" is to live in a "mist of confusion." Let's make it clear; there is no confusion regarding God's plan for your life as far as spiritual health, emotional health, and physical health is concerned. God wants you to walk in absolute liberty, health, and divine favor.

Today's Confession of Healing

I am the anointed of God. Divine favor rests upon me, and I walk in all of the benefits of His redemptive purposes in my life: spirit, soul, and body. I have been freed from the snares of the enemy, and I will be held captive no longer.

The welfare of the Gospel is mine, and I live my life by the fact that I have been delivered; I walk in supernatural clarity and divine restoration. All that the Father intended for my life is available to me in Christ, and I live daily in the blessing of the believer.

Day Fourteen

BLESS THE LORD, O MY SOUL

"Bless the Lord, O my soul, And forget not all His benefits, Who forgives all your iniquities, Who heals all your diseases, Who redeems your life from destruction, Who crowns you with loving-kindness and tender mercies, who satisfies your mouth with good things, so that your youth is renewed like the eagles."

Psalm 103:2-5

This passage is highly insightful regarding health, healing, and wholeness. The dynamic that we discover in these verses is one of relationship. God's gift of health and wholeness is an extension of His passion and His love for you. As the writer of this Psalm, David expresses his commitment to living a life of submission unto the Lord predicated on his adoration of Him. "I will bless The Lord, O my soul," out of my emotions, my passions, my appetites, and my desires. All that I am, spirit, soul, and body, will be dedicated to worshipping Him.

It's interesting that David connects His worship to the beneficial aspects of living for and serving the Lord. The word forget is to "ignore, cause to wither or cease to care". In other words, we must give priority to a life of worship and not relegate it to a once-per-week exercise or a random, casual approach whenever we need something from God. When worship becomes a lifestyle and flows freely from a submitted heart, the benefits of God also flow freely from the heart of God toward you.

Lessons of Faith

Forget Not His Benefits: What are the benefits of The Lord? He forgives me. He heals me. He redeems my life. He crowns me with loving-kindness. He satisfies me. He renews my youthfulness. The word "benefit" literally means "from the bounty" of God; He has recompensed me by salvation. I have been forgiven and redeemed and qualified for all of the benefits of the covenant of redemption, hallelujah.

To be redeemed is to be "bought back", and it begs the question of exactly "what" has been repurchased? Life. The Hebrew word for life is "chayah". Genesis 2:7, says; "Then the LORD God formed the man from the dust of the ground. He breathed the breath of life into the man's nostrils, and the man became a living person". The word "breathed" is the same word as life in Psalm 103:4... "chayah". So, God bought back the breath of His life. Chayah means the breath of prosperity, the breath of health, the breath of life; it is the impartation of God Himself. He has bought me back from the destruction that Satan intended for me and the course of doom that my life was on without Christ.

Crowned with Kindness: As if that wasn't enough, He crowned me with kindness and mercy and continues to satisfy me with good things and renews my life to youthfulness. To be crowned is literally to be "surrounded with." It's not a hit and miss with the Lord, but an intentional surrounding of His divine favor, blessing, health, and wholeness. In other words, the favor of the Lord and the blessing of the Lord protect me. Not just with His love, but also His mercy. All my life, I have heard that the mercy of God was "not getting what you deserve "...not in this passage. The mercy of God (racham) is the deep love of God and His tender affections. God is desperately and passionately in love with me and surrounds me with that love. The result is that I am living a satisfying life. I am fulfilled and enriched in my Father's excesses toward me, and I am renewed daily in health and wholeness.

Today's Confession of Healing

My life and passions flow out of my worship to the Lord. I was created to worship Him, and I am fulfilling that purpose. Today, I live in the benefits of The Lord.

I am forgiven, I am healed, I am redeemed, I am satisfied, I am renewed, in Jesus' Name. I am surrounded and protected by the divine favor of God, and the love of God flows to me and through me. I walk in health and wholeness as the perfect plan and intention of the Lord towards me.

Day Fifteen

GUARD YOUR HEART

"My son attend to my words; incline your ear to my sayings. Do not let them depart from your eyes; keep them in the midst of your heart, for they are life unto those that find them, and health to all their flesh. Keep your heart with all diligence, for out of it are the issues of life."

Proverbs 4:20-23

Throughout this book, you will discover that I repeatedly emphasize the source of health and healing that you need is not an issue of "praying and receiving" at the point of need. Nowhere do you ever see Jesus asking the Father to heal somebody in a particular situation, but instead, He released healing by His faith and the spoken word.

So, what is the source of healing? It's the transcendent anointing of God (the supernatural ability of God that transcends and exceeds your natural capacity and understanding) and the authority of God that has been invested into you as a believer. "I give you authority to trample on snakes and scorpions and to overcome all the power of the enemy; nothing will harm you." (Luke 10:19).

You don't have to plead with God for something that you already have, and you HAVE authority over sickness. Our passage for today confirms that.

Lessons of Faith

The Authority of Faith: A fundamental principle is that the authority you walk in is directly correlated to the intimacy you have with the Father. Your relationship with Him brings an increase in both the anointing and authority. While there is an inherent anointing and authority that is yours by making Jesus the Lord of your life, the level of increase results from your intentional, relational investment. You are *given* the measure of faith, but the *increase* of faith is your responsibility.

The Kingdom's entirety is built upon and established by the "law of God," the Word of God. Deciding to set yourself in agreement with what God says, how God thinks and living by the principles of what He has decreed is "attending to His Word" in your life. I love the word "incline." It specifically means to be intentional, to "bend" yourself in a particular direction, and to stretch yourself towards something. In other words, this is not a casual approach to what God is saying; but a red-hot, hungry pursuit for who God is, His Word, and His Spirit.

Hearing the Word: How many times have we just casually heard the Word sitting in church or listening to teaching, and it comes in one ear and out the other? That's not what this is about. Inclining your ear is not just hearing in the realm of the natural but receiving the Word by faith and allowing it to become a revelation to you. It's making a decision never to turn away from what you discover to be the truth of God's Word and not letting the devious ploys of the enemy dissuade you from the Word of health, healing, and wholeness.

Choose today to set your gaze steadfastly without wavering and without compromise. The Word becomes the filter through which you see, perceive and discern your life and the issues and circumstances of your life. Not through fear, not through worry, not through tradition, not through opinions, and not through religion. Allow the Word to be the "gatekeeper" and the "defender" of your life. The Word becomes the filter through which all of your thoughts, decisions, and reasoning must pass. Be careful to give constant heed to the Word.

Guard Your Heart: How do you set yourself to live like that? You must be careful to guard your heart. The Israelite's considered the heart to be the very "seat of man", the central core of who you are...mind, will, and your emotions. (The source of your intentions, your thoughts, your understanding, your purposes.) The very hub of your existence spins off of and is connected to this central understanding. Guarding your heart causes it to become good ground for the life and the spirit of the Word. It becomes a breeding ground for health that is biblically described as "Rapha," divine health, holy composure, soothing Presence...tranquility (peace).

Out of the midst of your "heart" (mind, will, emotions) flow the issues of life, godliness, and destiny. Out of your heart flows life, the breath of God breathed into Adam at creation, and that Jesus breathed into His disciples. It is the definitive source of life, the fountain of life, the origin of life, health, healing, wholeness, prosperity, favor. Life, health, healing, wholeness, prosperity, and favor are already on the inside of you. It will flow out of who you are, the combination of the anointing and authority. That's how you release healing and health. You have the spiritual right and authority to release what is already on the inside of you. By the way, the best time to embrace health is BEFORE you are battling sickness. Make your daily confession of health and wholeness.

Today's Confession of Healing

"I am passionate about the Word. I choose today to rise and incline myself towards the life of the Word and the light of the Word.

I am not moved by what I see, hear, think or feel, but choose to press the thoughts of disease, sickness, fear, cowardice, and intimidation through the "filter of life," the Word of God. I am walking in the divine revelation of God's Word, and I allow it to permeate my mind, will, and emotions and become the source of life for myself and others.

I am the redeemed of God, and as such, I am the healed of God, the blessed of God, and I am free from the devious ploys of the enemy that would attempt to convince me otherwise."

Day Sixteen

SIGNS THAT FOLLOW

"And these signs will follow those who believe: In My name, they will cast out demons; they will speak with new tongues; they will take up serpents; and if they drink anything deadly, it will by no means hurt them; they will lay hands on the sick, and they will recover."

Mark 16:17-18

There is a unique "trusting relationship" that God has with those who faithfully follow Him. He has empowered believers to function on the earth in a lifestyle that is relative to His will and releases His power and authority into the lives of broken and lost humanity. There is a tendency to refer to God's intervention as miraculous. According to our text today, the "signs" that follow believers mark who we are as disciples. These "signs" are to be present in disciples' lives and distinguish them from those who don't know God. In a world that doesn't know God, these signs are unusual occurrences that transcend nature's ordinary course. If you are paying close attention, that last phrase is divine insight. People will tell you all the time to "let nature take its course," but God's Word declares that how we live our lives as believers transcends the ordinary course of life and nature.

Lessons of Healing

The true Life of A Believer: What is that life? It's the life of a believer. What do you believe? God's Word promises life, health, peace, and blessing to those who believe. The Greek word "believe" is the word "pisteuo" and is a derivative of "pistis," which is translated as faith, or conviction, and a total commitment. So, whom are the transcendent signs following? Those walking in a conviction that God's Word is true and choose to embrace it with a total commitment, without wavering.

Do these signs accompany those who "pray and hope" that there might be some level of intervention if God so chooses and blesses us in a moment of response to an emotional pleading prayer? No. These signs follow those who walk in a deep and total commitment and operate in the "Name" of Jesus. That's not just evoking His name through prayer, it is much more than that. The name of Jesus is the authority of Jesus that operates in a believer's life by an intimate relationship. In other words, the level of authority that you have is correspondent to the level of intimate relationship that you have with the Father.

We are Not Begging Believers: How do you approach the demonic sickness and disease? You "cast" it out. The Word cast means to drive out, to send out, and to command with authority. This reinforces the thought throughout this book that healing results from standing in faith and standing on the Word. This is not posturing yourself before God and begging Him to do what He has already given you the authority to do. Demons are referred to as inferior beings and are always subject to the authority you have as a believer walking in full conviction, commitment, and relational authority. Sickness and disease can undoubtedly seem to loom larger than life and stand as a mountain before you, but God's Word declares that it is inferior to the authority that you possess in Christ.

So, where does that leave us when it comes to sickness? You rise, take authority over it and lay hands on the sick. The laying on of hands is an important, biblical point of contact. It means to release out of the source of life that is on the inside of you. It is unleashing the might, activity, and power of God. In studying this scripture, the context is that of a gulf between the person who is suffering from sickness and the healing virtue of God. The laying on of hands bridges that gulf and establishes a divine connection between the person suffering illness and the source of health and healing. The exciting promise found in today's scripture is that at the point of contact, the sick (void of needed strength) will recover, which means to lay firm hold of and to fully possess the purposes and the plans of God, which is always divine health.

Today's Confession of Healing

I am a believer and not a doubter. I am full of faith and conviction that God's Word is faithful, and He is determined to fulfill His purposes of life, health, and healing to others through me.

The transcendent anointing that results from the life of the Word is common in who I am and how I live. I am not a stranger to the anointing or the power of God operating in me and through me.

I am available to be used by the Lord in the lives of others who may be battling sickness or disease. I stand against the lies of sickness, disease and infirmity. I make no room for it in my life, my family, or in those to whom God has called me to minister. Out of relational authority, I address sickness from the depths of the river of life that flows in me and through me.

Day Seventeen

HE HEALED ALL.

"When the evening had come, they brought to him many that were possessed with devils: and he cast out the spirits with his word and healed all that were sick; That it might be fulfilled which was spoken by Esaias the prophet, saying, Himself took our infirmities, and bare our sicknesses."

Matt 8:16-17

Israel was stirred up. They had never seen a man like this man, Jesus. He not only *spoke* with authority, but he *demonstrated* the Word through the miraculous. It's important to note a couple of things in today's reading. First of all, notice that Jesus performed the miraculous through His *spoken* word. Health and healing are never a matter of being good enough or earning it. The miracle that you need is in your mouth. Speaking and declaring the Word into your situation gives birth to the purposes and intentions of God. Remember, God's Word is His will. The Greek word here for "word" is "logos," and it specifically refers to the mandate of God, the order and declaration of God, as well as a particular kind and style of speaking, a distinct doctrine and teaching. What does that mean? When it comes to your healing, you better _know_ that God desires to heal you, and you better be _armed_ with the doctrine and instruction

81

of the Word that will lead you into that healing. That's what this book is all about.

Lessons of Healing

Jesus is the Healer: "Therapeuo," He heals, He cures, and He restores to health. Ultimately, the desire of the Father goes beyond your healing and directly to your health. You shouldn't wait until you are fighting sickness or disease to stand on the Word. The best time to believe God for your health is before you get sick. Daily confess the Word over your physical body and your family. Stand on the Word every single day and declare what God says about you:" you are walking in divine health." Please notice that the will of God was manifested in that every single person was healed. Nobody was left out. I've heard it said that it's "not the will of God to heal everyone." I believe that this scripture debunks that nonsense. If it wasn't the will of God to heal everybody, Jesus would have had to pick and choose, but He didn't, and we know that He was never out of the will of God.

Sickness Is Illegal: When you study the Word instead of just reading it, you begin to glean insights that otherwise might escape you. This book is not a matter of opinion or denominational doctrine but an in-depth study of God's Word, allowing us to mine out the truths that are hidden therein. I want you to notice that Jesus healed the "sick." If you read that at face value, you might not catch the significance of that word, but if you break it down and study it, you discover something that you can use in the battles you face.

The word here is "kakos," to be "physically ill." But it means so much more than that. The context of this word is that sickness has wrongly invaded your body; it is improper and existing in your body illegally. In other words, your body is the "temple of God" and not designed to be a residence for sickness or disease. If it has attacked your body, it has no legal right to be there, and it is NEVER the will of God for it to be in your body. *"Well, brother, sometimes God puts sickness on you to teach you something or to put you in a situation where you can be a witness for Him."* Really? So, in this instance, every *single* person, without fail, was destined to be healed without it being the will of God that one person would have to deal with sickness to fulfill the will of God? That seems unlikely.

Jesus Healed All: What is happening here is that it IS the will of God that all be healed, and that's precisely what happened. It says that the Father's will was being "fulfilled," which means that God's perfect will was being performed, executed and, completed. Again, what was that will? That every person is healed through the ministry and accomplishments of Jesus. It was true then, and it's true now.

Jesus "took" our infirmities. He forcefully seized and laid hold of them to deliver His people from them. Hebrews 13:8 says that "He is the same, yesterday, today and forever." If it was His will then, it's His will today. He still wants to lay hold of your sickness and deliver you from it. The source of healing is always love. He loved us so much that He gave His life for us. Not only so that we might experience eternal life, but also that we might live lives of blessing, relationship, health, and healing.

Today's Confession of Healing

The days of my sickness are over. From this day forward, I declare that I walk in divine health, healing and wholeness. Out of His love for me, Jesus took all of my infirmities and all of my sicknesses upon Himself.

I no longer walk under the curse of sickness, and when it does attempt to attack my body, it does so illegally. It has no right to reside in the temple of the Holy Spirit.

I am the righteousness of God in Christ Jesus, and I walk in the confidence that it is always God's will to heal me and that I walk in health. I confess today that my family walks in health and wholeness, and we make no room for sickness in our bodies.

Day Eighteen

THE CALLED AND SENT OF GOD

"Then He called His twelve disciples together and gave them power and authority over all demons, and to cure diseases. He sent them to preach the kingdom of God and to heal the sick."

Luke 9:1-2

There are two essential things for you to remember: you are the "called" of God, and you are the "sent" of God. Your life has a divine purpose in both the calling and the sending of God, as well as a promise that accompanies both of those dynamics. The promise that we find in today's scripture is not limited to the twelve original disciples but is available to today's disciples as well; that's us. So, let's get this straight: I have a divine calling of God on my life, I have been given power and authority over the strategies of darkness, I have been given authority and ability to cure diseases, I have been sent to a broken world with a specific kingdom message and to bring health and healing to those that are sick.

Lessons of Healing

You Are Invited: As a believer, you live under the divine and supernatural invitation of the Lord to represent the King and His kingdom. Along with that invitation also comes the actual power and authority to represent the kingdom in authenticity. Your invitation is to invade the kingdom of darkness with the force and the message of the kingdom, which is always good news. What is that good news? You no longer have to be sick; you no longer have to be broke, in bondage, or under the rule and dominion of an enemy. The authority you have been given is the right and privilege to rule over the works of darkness on behalf of the King. That means that you no longer have to cower in fear, stand in confusion or become mired in a battle that can't be won. The war has already been won, and you are now the enforcer of the victory of that battle.

God's will is divine health: The reality is that many believers are living under the weight of sickness and disease, and many genuinely believe that it's God's will to do so. Nothing could be further from the truth. Jesus has specifically given you the power and the authority to cure diseases, which means to bring into "divine restoration." If sickness were remotely the will of God, Jesus would have risked setting Himself against God's will by sending His disciples to be agents of divine health. To understand the magnitude of our calling and sending, the word sent is "apostello," which is the same word from which Apostle is derived, and it means to set in "divine order." So, in other words, sickness and disease are "out of order." That means it's out of the context of God's will, and we have been given the authority to bring it back into order, back into God's will, which is wholeness.

The Rule of the Kingdom: The kingdom of God is the "dominion and rule of a king, to be subject to the authority and rule of that king." Whose rule and dominion are you living under? If you are tolerating sickness and disease, it's certainly not under the dominion of King Jesus. Nothing outside of God's will (sickness) is a part of the kingdom of God, thus would be considered out of order.

When we set ourselves to "accept" sickness or disease, we give it authority to embed or take root in our bodies. We must set ourselves against sickness and decide that it's not the will of God. It's out of order, and it is invading your body illegally. Take up your fight against it by declaring the Word and the will of God over it. You do not have to co-exist with disease. You have been given the authority to heal the sick and to walk in health and wholeness in your own body.

Don't settle for anything less than the absolute will of God in your life and body. According to the Word, you are an ambassador of wholeness, anointing, and are ordained to take the kingdom's message (health and wholeness) to the nations. Let that begin in your own body and your own home.

Today's Confession of Healing

I am called of God and have been sent with power and authority to establish the kingdom of God and to bring the divine order of God wherever I go.

I have a divine calling of God on my life; I have been given power and authority over the strategies of darkness. I have been given authority and the ability to cure diseases, and I have been sent to a broken world with a specific kingdom message. I am authorized to bring health and healing to those that are sick.

I rise today in faith and authority, and I speak to the lies of the enemy to be broken, I declare freedom, liberty, and health to those that are bound, and I set myself against the powers of darkness. I am an ambassador of wholeness, and I have been anointed to take the kingdom's message to the nations.

Day Nineteen

TEACHING AND PREACHING THE GOSPEL

"And Jesus went about all the cities and villages, teaching in their synagogues, and preaching the gospel of the kingdom, and healing every sickness and every disease among the people."

Matthew 9:35

Jesus was a man on a mission. He wasn't just wandering about Israel aimlessly and doing the works of the ministry whenever the opportunity arose. Far from it. Jesus had a very definite purpose and a divine intention. His divine assignment was to expose the works of the devil and, in doing so, to bring about freedom, deliverance, and healing to people whose lives had been ravaged by the lies of the enemy. He walked with authority, he talked with authority, and he exercised the authority of the kingdom whenever He encountered the works of darkness that were manifesting in people's lives, including sickness.

Lessons of Faith

He Healed All: Jesus went into every city and every village and, amazingly enough, healed <u>every</u> sickness and disease among them. Notice that His mission was to defeat the enemy's works, and He did that by healing the sick. I'm smart enough to know that if any form of sickness was from God that Jesus would have just left well enough alone in case He healed against the will of God, which obviously, He never did. I love that Jesus took the time to teach people, and it's also interesting to note that the teaching and preaching came before the healing.

Why is that important? Because He was taking the time to build up and encourage their faith so that they could continue to walk in health after the healing. To teach means to "impart instruction, to instill doctrine, to explain and expound the Word." He was arming the people with what they would need to continue walking in faith relative to God's will for their lives. He taught in the cities; He taught in the villages. He taught in their synagogues (churches).

Far too often, the doctrines in our churches become diluted and distorted, and we end up not sure if it's God's will to heal us or not. We are taught to pray that the "will of God" be done. Well, the good news is that the revealed will of God is that we walk in divine health, healing, and wholeness. You can stand on that in faith and speak that over your body with absolute confidence that it is always the will of God to heal you. You never have to doubt; you never have to waiver or even remotely entertain anything else. His Word declares it, and so can you.

The Good News: Jesus was preaching the Gospel (the good news) of the kingdom. The kingdom of God's rule and God's reign, where

He is Lord supreme and has ultimate dominion. Since the source (entry point) of sickness and disease was sin, the kingdom is a place where Jesus is Lord and sin, and *all* of its effects have been crushed under the weight of His authority and must bow its knee to His Name.

The kingdom is not a place where sickness and righteousness cohabitate; it's not a place where darkness and light live together in a passive, compromising relationship. In the kingdom, Jesus is Lord, and *every* sickness, every disease, every work of darkness must and will bow its knee to the authority and the name of Jesus, and to those who carry that name. We aren't people who live the same old life that we've always lived, but we've added a "religious element" to who we are. Quite the contrary, we have been called (commanded) out of darkness. Jesus seized and took ahold of the diseases of the enemy working against us, redeemed us to walk in power and authority, and equipped us to stand against all of the works of darkness. You are the redeemed of God.

Today's Confession of Healing

I am a person on a divine mission. I have been called out of darkness and into His marvelous light. I am a living recipient of "the blessing," and all of the attributes of redemption belong to me.

I do not have to live with sickness and disease, I no longer have to make room for the lies and strategies of the enemy that manifest in sickness, and I do not have to accept anything less than my Father's perfect will.

God's perfect will for my life is divine health, healing, and wholeness, and I walk in the authority of the kingdom. I command healing in my body today, and I live by the power of the Word in my life and my family.

I am what God says I am, and I am not moved by others' opinions or any report or lie that is contrary to the decreed will of God for my life.

Day Twenty

I AM THE LORD WHO HEALS YOU

"If you diligently heed the voice of the Lord your God and do what is right in His sight, give ear to His commandments and keep all His statutes, I will put none of the diseases on you which I have brought on the Egyptians. For I am the Lord who heals you."

Exodus 15:26

As I have stated before, healing is not something that is "up for grabs." God doesn't decide on the spur of the moment, the ardor of your request, the depth of your need, or how many people you rally to your prayer need whether or not you're going to be healed. Healing is a covenant promise given by a covenant God to a people who walk in covenant. And there you have it; the covenant is a two-way street, and nowhere is that made more evident than Exodus 15.

Lessons of Healing

The Voice of Healing: The call of God to His people is that they would set themselves to walk in understanding, consent, and agreement to His Word. His longing is that we would be a sensitive people to His Word's voice, which is the voice of divine health and healing.

When you fill your spirit, soul, and mind with the Word of Healing, the Voice of Healing becomes predominant over the voices of sin, sickness, and disease. Walking in covenant with the Word is to walk in the power of God's proclamation over you, which is the "law of healing." It is to walk lawfully according to the Word, to walk upright, straightforward and correct. In other words, there is no vacillating in terms of what you believe about God, what you believe about healing, or what you believe about the Word of God.

Divine Alignment: I am aligning both my sight and my hearing with the charge of the Lord, His commands, and His commission. He has appointed and ordained health, healing, and wholeness for those who walk in divine covenant and relationship with Him. The word "sight" is the Hebrew word "Ayin," which means to align your mental and spiritual faculties to what God has declared over you in His Word, it means that your alignment becomes a fountain and a spring of life to you.

Be On Guard: Keeping the statutes of the Lord is to preserve and to protect the Word in your heart, your mind, and your will. Be on guard. Take heed, beware of the voices that would try to persuade you of a doctrine that God is anything but your Healer. The diseases that the Egyptians are susceptible to are NOT your diseases. You are the redeemed of God and walk in the power of redemption, health, and healing.

The Egyptians (worldly and carnal) are people who are bound, defiled, polluted, weakened, and sick. The word means that they are confined and living in their hostilities. You are the divine heir of Adonai, of Jehovah, the One true God who has always existed and surrounds you with His great love, mercy, kindness, and grace. He declares of Himself that He is Jehovah-Rapha, the One who heals you, keeps you healthy, removes the distress from your life, and restores you to divine favor.

Today's Confession of Healing

I am a believer and not a doubter. I do not walk in fear but faith. I walk in divine covenant with the Father, who loves me deeply and has provided for my health, healing, and wholeness. I am secure in my covenant of health, and I am not susceptible to the diseases of the unbeliever. I have a "made up mind," and I incline my ear to the Voice of Healing and my eye to the Word of Healing.

I come into agreement with my Father, who declares of Himself that He is my Healer. I don't have to beg God to heal me because I have a covenant that appoints me to healing, and I have been ordained for health. The fountain of healing and the spring of life flow from my innermost being into every part of my physical body by redemption.

Day Twenty-One

THE LORD IS MY REFUGE.

"Because you have made the Lord, who is my refuge, Even the Most High, your dwelling place, No evil shall befall you, Nor shall any plague come near your dwelling; with long life will I satisfy him and show him my salvation."

Psalm 91:9-10, 16

There is a place of protection and shelter from the danger and the falsehoods of sin, sickness, and disease. Remember, sickness is a lie, and anytime it attempts to invade or has invaded your physical body, it only does so based on a lie and is attacking your body illegally. That place of protection or refuge is your relationship with the Lord and with the Word. It's that place that I must stand in, put my trust in, and the place where I find confidence and hope (expectancy). It's the "law of life," the "law of healing," and transcends the law of sin and death from which sickness originates. While I'm not saying that there is sin in your life and that's what's producing sickness, I am saying that your advantage against it is a place of intimacy with the Father and His Word.

Lessons of Healing

God is the source of health, healing, and wholeness: He is superior to, far above, and exalted over all sickness and disease. Every knee will bow to His authority, and every sickness must submit to the Name of the Most High. His dwelling place is an intimate relationship, a habitation where He is the divine and ultimate authority. In that place, there is no room for both the divine life of God and the lie of the enemy; sickness, distress, misery, calamity, or to be broken. No evil shall befall me.

That's my promise, and that's my covenant. This is a place that cancels the enemy's demonic appointments that are destined and designed for evil. Think of it. Pushing into the heart of God, walking in a place of confidence and expectancy before Him by His Word, not only produces life, healing, health, and wholeness in me but also serves to cancel out the assignments of the enemies against me.

God has a Plan: The enemy has a plan for my life, family, and family. That's the bad news, but the good news is that so does God. God's plan for me is to draw me to Himself in intimacy, cover me with His love and protection and deliver me from the calamity and brokenness that is the result of the assignment of the enemy against me.

The battle that we all face is the constant barrage of lies and onslaught of sickness and disease. Still, in those moments, I must cling to the power and the authority of the Word and the declaration of God over myself and my family that His law of life is the authority that I stand on, and I will not vacillate.

Today's Confession of Healing

I choose today to hide in the shadow of the Almighty, under the refuge of His love, His authority, and His covenant promises over me. His Word over me is my confident expectancy, and I decide today to live according to the law of life, which transcends the law of sin and death.

I command every lie of the enemy resulting in sickness or disease to bow its knee to the Name of the Most High, my God who is above all sickness, exalted over all disease and established in truth and power.

Day Twenty-Two

THE WELL-WATERED GARDEN

"And the LORD shall guide you continually, and satisfy your soul even in drought, and make fat your bones: and you will be like a well-watered garden, and like a spring of water, whose waters fail not."

Isaiah 58:11

Everything that you need to be a success in life and to walk in the divine plans and purposes of God in your life is already on the inside of you. He's called the "Anointing to live," and He's the third part of the Trinity, the Holy Spirit. The anointing of God is the *"supernatural enablement of God that exceeds your natural capacities and abilities."* The health and healing you need doesn't exist in the heavenlies, and you don't need God to somehow send it down to you in your moment of need. Health, healing, and wholeness are already on the inside of you. It's the attribute of the Person of Jesus by the Holy Spirit.

Lessons of Faith

That's the "watered garden" and the "spring of water" that Isaiah talks about in this scripture. The point is not that God waits and makes a decision at the moment of your need, and then it's a toss-up at best. He has ALREADY decided AND decreed His plans and purposes for you, and Jesus paid the price for your health and healing. He desires to lead and guide you all the days of life, no matter what you might face or encounter. He leads you by His Word, and that's why you must grasp the concept of His purposes BEFORE you encounter any kind of an attack from the enemy.

All of us have faced times when it seems that there is no word of the Lord and no sense of His provision in our lives. Those are "times of drought." Even in those times, God makes it clear that His longing is that you would be filled and satisfied and not come up empty. Even in the times of weariness, God says, "I want you to be fulfilled, satisfied, and having all of your desires met. I want you to be enriched and filled to overflowing". "I will satisfy your soul, even when you face a drought".

The Soul of Man: The "soul" of man is considered the central core of who you are and is the "seat of your appetites, emotions, and passions." As the focal point of your emotions and mental activity and the place from which your character is derived, it becomes essential that your "soul is satisfied" by the good things of the Word and that there is no void of understanding.

Unless you walk in a true sense of understanding in terms of God's purposes, you become highly vulnerable to the enemy, especially during times of attack. If you don't resolve (in advance) what God says about your situation, you become susceptible to losing your resolve. Your emotions, your appetites, your character, and your thought processes must be rooted in the truth of God's Word regarding you and your family.

The Well-Watered Garden: To be "fat" is a military terminology and means that God will equip you for war and make you strong for the purposes of rescue, deliverance, and freedom as it manifests in your physical body (bones). Even during drought and warfare or any type of onslaught of the enemy, God has determined that you will be watered abundantly. The Hebrew word is "Ravah," and it means to be overflowing and saturated even to the point of being "drunk." You are a watered garden producing life, health, and wholeness, surrounded and covered by the Word of the Lord, Himself.

God says that He will cover and defend you in the same way that He surrounded the Garden of Eden with His grace, life, and presence. Not only that, but the Lord declares that you, yourself, will become a source of life flowing from the very words of your mouth. You will become a *Spring of Water*, and life will flow from the very command of your words. Does that sound like a beat-up, defeated, nominal person who's just barely getting by and is susceptible to every wind that blows? I think not.

That sounds like a mighty man or woman of God walking in life, victory, and success; that sounds like YOU.

Today's Confession of Healing

I am not defeated, broken, or beat down. I am mighty in God, and the Streams of Living Water flow in me and through me. I possess the very source of life, health, and wholeness in my being.

God supernaturally leads me through the deserts of life by the Word of Life that flows in me and by the anointing of God. Even during times of drought, I am enriched, filled to overflowing, and satisfied by the life of the Word.

God's purposes towards me cover and saturate me, and I walk in the freedom in who I am and who I am becoming.

Day Twenty-Three

HE SENT HIS WORD

"He sent His word and healed them and delivered them from their destructions."

Psalm 107:20

God, Himself, is the very essence of healing, health, and wholeness. He is much more interested in your health and wholeness than He is in your healing. The pursuit of healing indicates disease, while wholeness is the absence of disease, which is God's will and plan for your life. In Exodus 15, God makes a strong statement relative to Egypt's diseases and plagues (representation of the sensual world and its kingdom of which the prince of darkness currently rules over). God emphatically states that He will not allow any of those diseases to come upon you and declares of Himself that He is Jehovah-Rapha, the Lord, your Healer.

Lessons of Healing

He Sent His Word: In Psalm 107:20, a foundation of healing, health, and wholeness is once again established, "I sent My Word and healed you." The word "sent" is the Hebrew word "Shalach" and means to be a direct extension, to be "stretched out." The power of health and healing is God, literally extending the essence of who He is directly to you through His provision of healing. Jesus was "stretched" out on your behalf, receiving stripes upon His body to redemptively secure your "rights" to walk in divine health.

Not only has God extended the rights of health, healing, and wholeness to you, but He also established the power of His Word over you, the Word that defines who He is AND who you are, the healed of God. "Dabar" is Hebrew for "word" and refers to the declaration of God over you.

God provided for your healing, when He "commanded" and "declared" it over you. God's investment of Himself as "Jehovah-Rapha" not only provides for your physical health but deliverance and supernatural release from the effects and stresses that poor health may have had on you.

Today's Confession of Healing

According to the Word and the provision that Jesus made for me, I declare (even as God does) that I have every right to divine health, healing, and wholeness. I walk in the redemptive essence of who God is in my life: spirit, soul, and body.

Day Twenty-Four

SPEAKING TO YOUR MOUNTAIN

"So Jesus answered and said to them, "Have faith in God. For assuredly, I say to you, whoever says to this mountain, 'Be removed and be cast into the sea,' and does not doubt in his heart, but believes that those things he says will be done, he will have whatever he says."

Mark 11:22-23

Today, I want to shock your senses with a statement that you will not hear very often but is instrumental in equipping you to move forward with an accurate understanding of how to walk in divine health and healing. "Your need does not move God, and He does not respond to your lack." Does that mean God is not compassionate? Not at all. It means that the kingdom operates on the principle and law of the Word of God, and it was out of His compassion that He made a way available for your need to be met and for you to be healed. What, then, does move God? It's your faith and your obedience. If you rise with a level of capacity that can effectively stand against the lies of sickness and disease, it will be because you *develop* your faith.

Lessons of Healing

Faith Comes by Hearing: Romans 10:17 says that "faith comes by hearing the Word of God." Faith is not a religious emotion or a wish and a hope that God "might do something" if He chooses. Faith is a deep and abiding conviction which is the result of hearing the Word of God. You must understand this is not a casual hearing of the Word that goes in one ear and out the other.

Your natural ear is only the beginning point of hearing the Word. The Greek word for hearing is "akoe," and it means to receive instruction, give specific attention to, perceive, comprehend, and develop an understanding. Faith is the result of a person who has an insatiable hunger for the Word and allows it to penetrate their heart. It consumes their thoughts, dictates their passions, mandates their desires and appetites, and is the primary source of shaping their will and character. That's the level of faith that Jesus was referring to when He said, "have faith in God."

The Release of Faith: Your mountain is not going away on its own. It's not going to crumble away by natural erosion; you must get aggressive with it. Faith _comes_ by naturally hearing the Word and allowing it to become supernatural on the inside of you. It is _released_ by the natural words of your mouth and becomes a supernatural weapon against that which has risen against you and is contrary to God's will.

To speak to your mountain is to affirm the Word, to maintain your posture of the Word, and to release the command of the Lord against your mountain. It is standing without wavering or relenting, no matter what it may look like in the natural. The command of the Lord is that your mountain *will* be removed; in other words, take it by force and, by doing so, cause it to cease its activity.

When Jesus spoke of the mountain being cast into the sea, the word He used was in reference to the "Red Sea." Any Israelite that heard that would have automatically thought of the defeat of the Egyptian Army. That's the effect of your faith. The mountain that has risen against you will ultimately be defeated and wind up at the bottom of the Sea along with the Egyptian army.

Do Not Doubt: The critical aspect of this scripture is that you do not "doubt" in your heart. Once you stand on the Word, the enemy will tempt you with your feelings, what you hear others say about your situation and the fact that your breakthrough didn't happen overnight.

No matter what you may think, hear, see or feel, you must not withdraw or dispute what God says about your situation. Be careful not to allow others to cause you to contend against the Word or to hesitate to believe what the Word says. Walk in your confidence and be "fully persuaded and confident of this, that he who began a good work in you will carry it on to completion until the day of Christ Jesus." Philippians 1:6.

Today's Confession of Healing

I am being shaped, fashioned, and developed by the Word of God. My faith is being strengthened daily, and I am passionate about the Word.

I allow the Word to consume my thoughts, become my passion, and mandate the desires and appetites of who I am. I speak with authority to my mountain.

I stand against illegal sickness and rise against it in the Name of Jesus. No matter what my situation looks like or what I might feel, God's Word is truth, and I am the healed of God.

I walk in divine health, healing, and wholeness all the days of my life. I am confident and fully expectant that the work that has begun in me will come to full maturity.

Day Twenty-Five

TRUST IN THE LORD

"Trust in the Lord with all your heart, And lean not on your own understanding; In all your ways acknowledge Him, And He shall direct your paths. Do not be wise in your own eyes; Fear the Lord and depart from evil. It will be health to your flesh and strength to your bones".

Proverbs 3:5-8

Walking in the covenant blessing of God has always been directly correlated to your relationship with Him. The degree that you have intimacy with the Father, is the degree to which you will walk in authority, in covenant blessing, and experience all of the benefits of that covenant, including physical healing.

There is a confident expectancy that arises in your spirit when you are intimate with the Lord. You are safe, secure, and protected. When the lies of disease and sickness confront you, you are NOT MOVED. In this passage of scripture, we are directly instructed not to be led by our human understanding and intellect, but to resolve to stand on the declaration of the Word of healing over us.

Lessons of Healing

In all your ways, acknowledge Him: I have to spend a few moments on this statement because it says so much more than what you might derive just by simply reading it. The word "ways" (darak) is a military term that means to tread. It's the same word that God used when He spoke to Joshua and promised that He would give him every place upon which his feet "tread." In other words, where you exercise spiritual authority, that's where you will find victory and possession. The key to understanding is that your authority results from your "acknowledgment" of God, which means to have intimacy (yada) with God. Whenever you face sickness or disease, it's not a time to start whining and worrying; it's time to fight with the covenant authority you have as a believer.

Jehovah-Rapha: The Lord declares that when you walk in that place, He will make your journey straight. The word "straight" literally means to be upright, just, and lawful. What does that mean? It implies that sickness and disease are unlawful, illegal, and outside of the bounds of God's plan and intention for you and that He has made provision for you to live according to the law of health, healing, and wholeness. The Word is healing (Rapha) to your body and refreshment to your bones. Rapha is the investment of the very healing essence of God Himself into the entirety of your being, as well as the restoration of divine favor.

The picture here is based on the word "flesh" (shor), which means umbilical cord. As a child receives health, life, nourishment, and sustenance in the womb from the mother as it flows from the umbilical cord, you are connected directly to the Father through a "spiritual umbilical cord," and the health, life, nourishment, prosperity, wholeness, and refreshment flows directly from Him into you.

Not only that, but as it "strengthens" your bones, there is a literal refreshing (shaqah), which means to drink from a fountain. Hallelujah. I'm drinking from the fountain of health, of life, of nourishment that flows directly from my relationship with my Father.

Today's Confession of Healing

I walk in the benefits of covenant blessing because I walk in intimacy with my Father. I am not moved by what I see, think, hear or feel. I have a confident expectancy that as I am relationally connected to the Lord, I am safe, secure, and drinking from the fountain of health and wholeness.

Day Twenty-Six

THE WORD THAT GOES FORTH.

"So shall my word be that goes forth out of my mouth: it will not return unto me void, but it will accomplish that which I please, and it shall prosper in the purposes for which I sent it."

Isaiah 55: 11

God has spoken His Word. His declarative Word established the world, its boundaries, and its principles. By His Word, all things were made, and all things have been brought into divine destiny and order, including your life and all that concerns you. Your life is not up for grabs, and your future is not left up to the random occurrences of life and especially not to the lies of the enemy. The Word of the Lord covers you, and you are secure in what God says about you.

In today's reading, the decisive declaration of the Lord is that His Word over you will accomplish all that it has been intended to accomplish and that you will live in the fruit and the blessing of the Word. The lesson to be learned is to use our mouths' words effectively, even as God does. He spoke the Word as a command, and so should you.

Lessons of Healing

The Authority is Yours: You have the authority to stand on the Word as a divine promise and to release it over your life's circumstances and the challenges that you might face. God's Word always comes forth with a distinct purpose, and there is no shadow of doubt or wavering. Rise speak the Word with confidence that what God says about anything in your life is His absolute will, purpose, and plan, and whenever you express it in faith, He will stand behind you what you declare.

Whenever you speak the Word, you're not even speaking your desires, but you are releasing the Father's desires into whatever you are facing. His Word is ALWAYS His will. It's interesting to note that the word for going forth, "yatsa," is in the context of deliverance. In other words, God says that when I speak my Word over your life, it's for your redemption and freedom.

When you combine the thoughts of releasing the word and it not returning as void, it paints a picture of the Word that goes forth in the power of deliverance. The result is restoration, refreshing, and repair, causing the enemy to relinquish his grip on your life. In other words, ALL that the enemy has stolen from you will be taken back and restored to its original intention, plan, and purpose. It speaks explicitly of spiritual relations and human relations as well as your physical health. The Good News is that Jesus made way for your divine well-being; spirit, soul, and body.

The Appointed Word of Healing: You must rise today and stand on the promise that His Word will not return void but that it will accomplish the very purpose for which it is sent. The Word of the Lord has been appointed, established, and instituted on your behalf so that God's divine will come to fruition in all that concerns you. The enemy wants you to walk in the lie that you are barely getting by and that God's purposes are for somebody else and not for you. NOTHING could be further from the truth. This is your Word, this is your promise, you are EVERYTHING that God has declared over you, and you have every right to claim every guarantee of the Word for yourself and your family. Your life is NOT up for grabs, and, according to this scripture, you have been appointed to blessing, victory, and life. It's the desire and the pleasure of God that you walk in His blessing; determine today that you will do precisely that.

Today's Confession of Healing

It doesn't matter what it looks like, what it feels like, or what I hear. I AM what God says I am, and I have what He says I have.

My life operates by the divine order of the Word, and I will not settle for anything less. My life and my physical body are not up for grabs or prone to the lies of sickness and disease. Any physical ailment that attempts to attack my body does so illegally, and I rise and judge it by the Word of healing and the provision of the cross.

The Word that has been declared over me is strong and effective and establishes God's perfect plan and purpose in which I am becoming; spirit, soul, and body.

Day Twenty-Seven

SEEK AND YOU WILL FIND.

"Ask, and it shall be given to you; seek, and you shall find; knock, and it shall be opened unto you. For every one that asks receives; and he that seeks finds; and to him that knocks it shall be opened. Or what man is there of you, whom if his son asks for bread, would he give him a stone? Or if he asks for a fish, will he give him a serpent? If you then, being evil, know how to give good gifts to your children, how much more shall your Father which is in heaven give good things to them that ask him?"

Matt 7:7-11

Throughout this book, the common theme is that healing, health and wholeness are all a part of the redemptive provision purchased for us by Jesus. In today's reading, the context is that of our salvation and all that accompanies it. As a believer, it is important that you walk in knowledge and understanding of exactly what Jesus purchased for you and the rights that you have as a believer. The Greek word for salvation is "sozo", and it literally means "total salvation for total man," which is spirit, soul and body.

Jesus paid the total price that you might walk in the blessing of redemption spiritually, emotionally and physically.

Lessons of Healing

God has already Healed You: I've heard people teach this scripture that if you don't get what you need from God, you just keep on knocking, keep on asking and eventually, you'll wear the Lord down and He'll give you what you desire. That's nonsense. In this scripture, God is saying that He has already given you everything that you need to walk in this life as the redeemed of God. Whenever you are facing sickness or disease, you don't have to beg God to heal you...He already has. You don't have to beg God to bless you, He already has, you don't have to beg Him to deliver you, He already has.

The word "given" here is the Greek word "didomi" and it means to "bestow" upon somebody and to "furnish and supply all things necessary. He has literally committed to you His promise of life and health. This scripture isn't telling us to "beg from God", but it is enforcing that His promises are yours through salvation. When you became His child, all of the rights, privileges and authority to walk in divine blessing became yours, your job now is to enforce the law whenever the enemy tries to cross that line and tempt you with anything less than what God has already said about you.

If you "seek" God, you *will* find Him: God isn't playing hide and seek...He *wants* you to find Him. This word promises us that we will walk in a new sense of discovery and understanding and that through practice and experience, we will begin to walk in the knowledge of how to acquire, obtain and procure the promises of God for ourselves. In other words, to "find" God is not to know about Him, or to hear about Him from others, but to personally experience that His Word is true. His Word will not be denied, and He is faithful to His Word to perform it.

How then do you practically walk in these promises? Thanks for asking. That's where the word "receives" comes in. Just as you had to "receive" the free gift of salvation, you must also receive your healing, your peace, and your deliverance. Again, let's visit the Greek word to see what we can find…the word receive is "lambano" and it's a very important word to understand. It means to "lay ahold of, to apprehend, to seize, to take possession of, to appropriate to one's self and to obtain". It's not a sense of "let's wait and see what happens" or "I'm just hoping and praying that maybe God will heal me," not at all.

This word is about recognizing, understanding and embracing the promises and the provisions of your redemption and making a decision to walk in and embrace them regardless of what you see, hear, think or feel. This is an active faith that reaches out and demonstratively takes hold of the promise and stands on it without wavering or doubt.

In fact, the bread that is referenced here has specific roots to the table of the Lord, which represents the broken body that Jesus suffered specifically so that you might walk in divine health and healing. Rise up today, stand on the Word, declare the Word to your body, to your circumstances and lay hold of the promises that are yours.

Today's Confession of Healing

I am a child of the most High God. I am a believer and not a doubter. Today, I confess that I walk in the full provision of redemption in every area of my life: spirit, soul and body.

My Father is delighted to make me a recipient of every good thing that comes from Him and I'm honored to walk in it. I chose to live by virtue of what God says I am and have, and not by the opinions of others or even of my own flesh.

I walk in the understanding and the authority of the Word. I lay hold of the promise of health and wholeness without wavering or doubting. God has already healed me and today I appropriate by faith, that which has been accomplished on my behalf.

Day Twenty-Eight

YOUR LIGHT SHALL BREAK FORTH

"Then your light shall break forth like the morning, your healing shall spring forth speedily, And your righteousness shall go before you; the glory of the Lord shall be your rear guard."

Isaiah 58:8

In the very depth of who you are, deep in the wellspring of your spirit, is the anointing of health. Many people make the common mistake of coming to the Lord in a prayer posture requesting healing at their time of need. In actuality, the source of healing is already on the inside of you; it's the anointing to live, living out of the abundance of the life of God that is your redemptive right.

It is in that time of need that your "light shall break forth". Describing the prosperity of health and the Word's instruction, Isaiah encourages us to allow the healing directives of the Word to take precedence. Begin to declare the word of healing, stand in faith on the word of wholeness and let the light of the word break forth in power and authority over the sickness that is illegally attempting to invade your body.

Your healing shall spring forth speedily: The Hebrew word for healing in this passage is "arak" and means to bring increase to your days of life. In other words, the curse is reversed. That which the enemy meant for your demise and destruction, the Word of health rebukes and by that word brings and releases out of your spirit, the abundance of life and restoration to the purposes of God over you.

Many times, I have said that God is more interested in your health than your healing. This passage introduces the concept of an approach to proactive health instead of relying upon healing once you are sick. "Your righteousness shall go before you." The word "before" is the Hebrew word "panah," which means to clear the way or to make clear.

In other words, God will establish your health before it even becomes an issue. Only eternity will reveal how many times sickness and disease was circumvented on your behalf, and you never even knew about it. The provision has been made, allowing you to put that confession in your arsenal. Confess your health daily. Don't wait until you are fighting sickness to begin declaring the Word over your physical body. It's easier to "stay healthy" than it is to fight sickness.

Today's Confession of Healing

Father, I thank You that according to Your Word, I am ALREADY the healed of God. I walk in the divine health and wholeness that was invested in me by my salvation. My righteousness in Christ goes before me and rebukes sickness and disease BEFORE it even has a chance to invade my body. My health is a covenant right established by the sacrifice of Jesus, and I am what the Word says I am.

Day Twenty-Nine

HEALING IN HIS WINGS

"But for those of you that fear my name shall the Sun of righteousness arise with healing in His wings, and you shall go forth and grow up as calves of the stall. And you shall tread down the wicked; for they shall be ashes under the soles of your feet in the day that I shall do this, says the LORD of hosts."

Malachi 4:2-3

God is bringing you to a renewed place of walking in the authority of the Word, and a fresh understanding of who He is, His principles, and His life as it operates in you and through you. You are being established in a new place of reverence, honor, respect, and awe that is releasing new confidence in who you are and how you approach your life issues. From that renewed place of life, the Lord promises that His righteousness will shine upon you and surround you on every side, even as the sun shines upon the land.

Lessons of Healing

Healing of the Redeemed: The word righteousness (Tsdaqah) is the righteousness that results from our salvation. You are the redeemed of God, *"let the redeemed say so"*. My redemption means that God has fully justified me; I walk in health, healing, and prosperity as well as the blessing. He is my covering, He is my delight, and He is my health, my life, and my righteousness. His righteousness permeates every arena of who I am: spirit, soul, and body.

Notice that the healing virtue was found in His wings. The historical passage that is being referenced here is found in Numbers 15:37-41, *"The Lord said to Moses, speak to the Israelites and say to them: throughout the generations to come, you are to make tassels on the corners of one's garments, with a blue cord on each tassel. You will have these tassels to look at and so will remember all the commands (the Word) of the Lord, that you may obey them and not prostitute yourselves by going after the lusts of your hearts and eyes. Then you will remember to obey all my commands and will be consecrated to your God. I am the Lord your God."*

Wings of Healing: So, what does that mean to us? The tassels (the wings) represent the Word of God and your obedience and submission to the Word. Another excellent example of this is found in Matthew 9:20-22 when the woman with the issue of blood touched the "hem of His garment." She knew exactly what she was doing; she was laying hold of the Word of healing, the promise of the Lord in terms of her health. In the moment of your crisis, what will you do?

Will the report of the doctor, move you? The whispers of fear from those around you, the opinion of well-intended but biblically ignorant religious people, or will you grab ahold of the wings, the hem of the garment, and stand on the authority of the Word that declares over you that you are the healed of God? The word "healing" here is a derivative of the word Rapha (Jehovah-Rapha, "the Lord, our Healer"); it's stronger than our typical thought of being healed but means that which was considered by man; to be incurable, is now healed.

Your destiny is not one of dwelling in adverse circumstances, hoping and longing for something you will never have. Your future is to move forward in faith and to "go forth." This phrase means to live your life with purpose and a sense of divine destiny, to see the enemy crushed beneath your feet, regardless of the lies you might be facing or the battle in which you might be engaged.

Today's Confession of Healing

I walk in a clear understanding of the Word and the authority that I have as a believer. I stand in the strength and the promise of the Word that I am the healed of God. Jesus is my covering, my delight, my health, my life, and my righteousness.

Every arena of who I am: spirit, soul, and body is covered by His grace and His promise and provision. Today, I lay hold of the strength, the power, and the authority of the Word, and no matter what I see, hear, think or feel, I am not moved by anything other than the declaration of His Word over me.

I chose today to move forward in faith, to live my life with purpose, and I WILL see the enemy and all of his lies crushed beneath my feet.

Day Thirty

YOUR WORD IS SETTLED

"Forever, O LORD, Your Word is settled in heaven. Your faithfulness endures to all generations; you established the earth, and it abides. They continue this day according to your ordinances, for all are your servants. Unless your law had been my delight, I would then have perished in my affliction. I will never forget your precepts, for, by them, you have given me life.
I am yours, save me."

Psalm 119: 89-94

As you have worked through this book, the one thing that I have stressed over and over again is that "healing is always the will of God in every single situation." That doesn't mean that every person is always healed. That is an entirely different scenario, and questions remain as to why some people do not experience their earthly healing. Only God can answer those questions. However, that does not put us in a situation where we have to second-guess the Word of God. God's Word is never relative, and it is never subjective. His Word and His authority are always absolute, enduring, and never changing.

Lessons of Healing

His Word is forever settled in Heaven: The Word of God is the promise of God and the covenant of God towards His children. It is a Word that has a continual and never-ending existence and does not waiver no matter what the situation. It's not God's will to heal one person, but not His will to heal another. It is always His will to heal every person walking in the covenant right of healing as a born-again child of God. What He has promised in His Word is appointed, fixed, and established both in heaven and on the earth without compromise. He is a God of fidelity and steadfastness, and His Word is without question and not up for debate. His Word has been established with the specific intentions of fulfilling His covenant and His will on the earth towards His children.

The Law of the Kingdom: It's important to remember that the kingdom of God is established upon the law and operates by the principles of that law. In this scripture, that law is referred to as the "ordinances of God," which means that they have been "legally judged and decided upon." In other words, the covenant promises that you walk in and read in the Word aren't just some religious garble; they are the law of God that has withstood the test of time and will not bend nor bow to whatever lie you might be facing.

His Word is life, truth, health, and wholeness, legally. Why do I point that out? Because Satan knows it, and so should you. These words you are reading in the scripture aren't just the sweet, religious musings of a Psalmist. This is a legal, binding, eternal covenant spoken and declared by God, who cannot break the covenant. This Word is forever settled. You must read the fine print on any contract (covenant), but the enemy is banking on you *not* reading, *not* knowing, and *not* being informed.

He knows that he has *no* legal right to invade your body with sickness, but if he can get you to open the door or accept it, he will gain that ability by a lie. Any sickness that is invading your body is there illegally, and you have the covenant and legal right and authority to command it to leave your body. Listen to what the Word says, and this is my paraphrase, but not taken out of context; "only when your Word is not my delight and only when I forget your precepts, do I perish in my affliction."

So, when the Word becomes my delight (the object of my attention), and the command of God becomes that which I build my conviction on, my trust, and my confidence, I will not go astray, and I will not be destroyed. I will not be the subject of suffering and oppression that is brought upon me by the hand of the enemy.

The Breath of Life: It is by the Word that the very life of God is breathed into your spirit, soul, and body. "*By your precept, you have given me life*". The word life is the same word used for God's breath that He breathed into Adam and caused him to become a living being. It's the breath of "Chayah," the breath of God that brings prosperity, health, wholeness, restoration, and favor. The Psalmist concludes this scripture by saying: "I am Yours, save me." This is a great word that you need to become familiar with. It's the word "yashah," meaning to save. But it's so much more than that; it means to "save us, heal us, prosper us and deliver us."

Every year, at the conclusion of the Feast of Tabernacles, all of Israel would gather at the temple with their palm branches and make this declaration..." yashah-nah." Save us NOW, heal us NOW, prosper us NOW, and deliver us NOW. Our modern word "Hosanna" is the word "yashah-nah." The Jewish people were taught that Jesus would come riding into Jerusalem riding on a lowly colt. When the crowds saw Jesus riding into Jerusalem, it all came into focus, and they began to shout, waving the palm branches and making their declaration of "yasha-nah.

The Messiah is our savior, our healer, our deliverer, and the one who causes us to prosper. They knew and understood that covenant right was theirs and that the fulfillment of it would come through the Messiah, and so it has. Israel has been blinded to the truth and the power of the Messianic covenant, but it's true today for those who choose to put their faith and their trust in Jesus as their Messiah. Make your declaration today, "yashah-nah".

Today's Confession of Healing

Today, I stand on the covenant truth that healing is the children's bread. It is always and only the will of God that I walk in divine health, healing and wholeness.

I resist the lies of the enemy that says I have to be sick, and I command divine health to flow into my physical body. I command the full manifestation of the reality of the kingdom in my body today. Jesus paid the redemptive price that I might walk in wholeness, and I refuse to settle or live with anything less than what He purchased for me.

Any sickness that attacks my body or my family is a lie, and its invasion is illegal. I judge it as such and declare that Jesus is Lord over my body and my family and "by His stripes, I am healed."

I walk in power and authority of the commands and the precepts of the Lord, and today I shout Hosanna, "Yashah-Nah," save me NOW, heal me NOW, prosper me NOW, deliver me NOW, in Jesus' Name.

Day Thirty-One

FOR GOD WAS WITH HIM

"How God anointed Jesus of Nazareth with the Holy Spirit and with power, who went about doing good and healing all who were oppressed by the devil, for God was with Him."

Acts 10:38

Jesus is the Christ, the Messiah, and the Anointed One. While He was on the earth, He never operated as a member of the Godhead but limited Himself as the "son of man." Had Jesus functioned in the capacity of the Godhead, He would have forfeited His right to be the redemptive sacrifice for humanity. All that He accomplished through His life was by the "anointing," the "supernatural enablement of God that exceeds your natural capacity." While He was on the earth, He only did God's will that was revealed to Him, and He is *still* doing the will of God through His body, the church. Notice that the will of God was to heal "all" who were oppressed.

Lessons of Healing

Sickness is Not of God: Without exception, healing was the will of God when Jesus was on the earth, and it is still the will of God today. From this scripture, we can deduce that God's will is always good, and that Jesus only did what was good. That's a reminder to us that

God doesn't have to use evil to accomplish His will or His purposes on the earth. Sickness is never good, and it is never God. In the context of this scripture, the word "good" means that the life of Jesus was spent releasing the benefits of the covenant...and obviously, that includes healing and freedom from oppression that originates from the devil.

The oppression of the enemy is harsh and unrelenting. Proverbs 17:22 says that *"a cheerful heart is good medicine, but a crushed spirit dries up the bones."* That's the heavy-handed oppression of the enemy that crushes and drains your hope of life and "dries up the bones," which is a weakening of the nerves, the drying up of the marrow of the bones, emaciating the body and reducing it to an unhealthy skeleton. It's also another term for rheumatoid arthritis. None of those things are the will of God for your life, and you have every covenant right to stand against them.

Jesus Triumphed over Sickness: Jesus not only went about healing all and doing good, but Colossians 2:15 says that *"having disarmed principalities and powers, He made a public spectacle of them, triumphing over them in it."* When Jesus "disarmed" the powers of darkness, he stripped them of their "right" to oppress you with sickness, affliction, and disease.

He took away their power and their authority, leaving only the power of the lie. That's important for you to remember. If the enemy is going to trap you, it will be because of a lie. The triumph of Jesus over the power of darkness is your health and wholeness, accomplished on your behalf on the cross of Calvary. Healing is one of the benefits of redemption, it belongs entirely to you, and the Father is pleased when you lay hold of His promise of healing to you and appropriate it by faith.

Today's Confession of Healing

Jesus paid the ultimate price on my behalf so that I would not have to be tormented by the oppressive hand of the enemy.

God is good, and all of His plans and purposes for me are good. He delights in my health and wellbeing and longs to see me living in the fullness of the redemptive benefits provided for me at Calvary.

All of the powers and principalities have been disarmed and stripped of their rights to oppress me with sickness, disease, or affliction. I rise and resist the lie and stand in the power and authority of the Word of God over my life.

ABOUT THE AUTHOR

Scott Reece is a man who is passionate about the Word of God. With thirty-seven years of ministry experience, he has served as a youth pastor, planted a church and served as a denominational executive for thirteen years in the Southeastern United States.

As a father of six children, his longing is to see the next generation rise up and embrace the truth and integrity of the Word of God and change the world through the Word.

Made in the USA
Monee, IL
02 April 2021